Stars

Foreword

In September 2016 I was asked by my friend, Ben Read, to give a public lecture at the Tetley arts centre in the northern English city of Leeds on my father, the artist Stass Paraskos. The Tetley was showing an exhibition of paintings by Stass, originally exhibited in Leeds in 1966, in a now notorious show called Lovers and Romances. The original 1966 display had been raided by the police and my father subsequently charged, under the Vagrancy Acts of 1823 and 1838, and the Obscene Publications Act 1953, with showing images likely to corrupt and deprave anyone who viewed them.

My initial response to Ben's request was to refuse. At that point I had written on my father twice following his death in 2014,[1] and my feeling was that it was time for other people to speak on him, particularly people who could muster a sense of academic detachment from the subject in a way that is, inevitably, impossible for me. However, Ben would not take no for an answer, and so I gave a talk on my father and the 1966 Leeds court case, and everyone involved seemed pleased. Yet, a similar dilemma faces me now in writing this essay on Stass.

As a professional writer on art I know the pitfalls in relying on subjective family reminiscences as an art historical resource, and as one of Stass's children I also know the emotional drain that comes from reliving memories, even when they might be happy ones. My personal inclination is always to try to move forward, rather than constantly reliving the past, and so this essay presents me with a dilemma, whether to write it, or to try again to say no. But, as you will have guessed by now, I have not said no.

In any celebration of an artist's life and work I think it is important to get across the full breadth of that life, and the philosophical underpinnings of their work. Perhaps these are impossible ambitions to set oneself, but I will try at least to make a start.

Dr Michael Paraskos
Lecturer in art history, Imperial College London

1. These were in the novel In Search of Sixpence, published in 2016; and in the Cyprus art magazine, Cyprus Dossier, issue 8, published in 2015

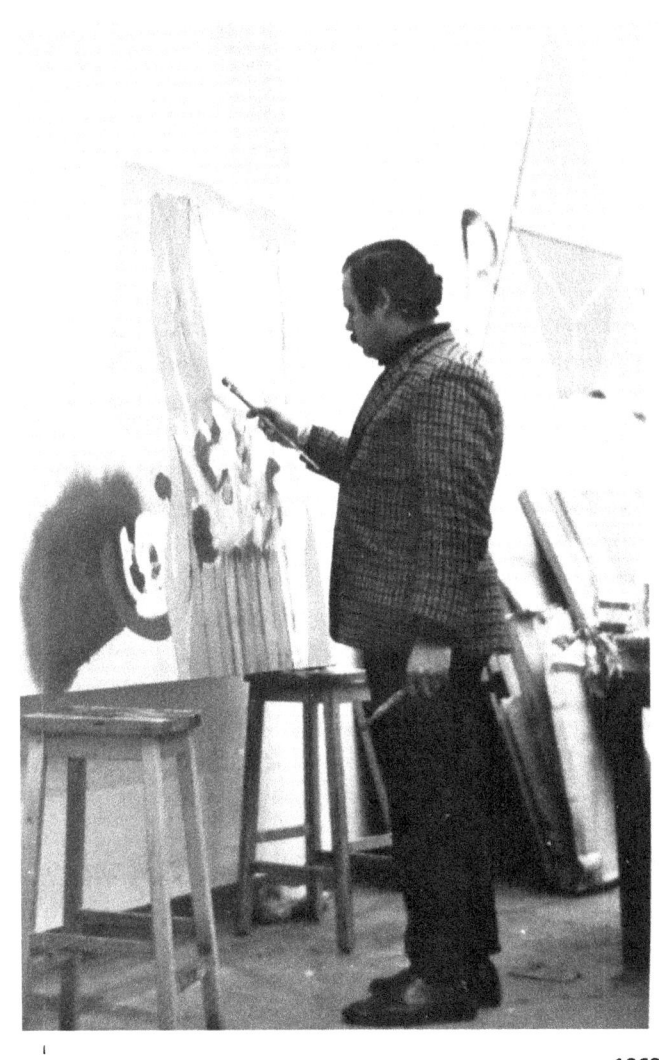

1968
Stass Paraskos at his studio in Leeds

Stass Paraskos: A Celebration

In terms of the philosophical underpinning of Stass's work, it is useful to think of Stass's teaching methods, which were not divorced from his own studio practices, but derived from them. Often Stass would tell students that they need to create tension in their work, which did not mean an emotional sense of fear or unease, but a visual phenomenon. Most artists want to create images that are balanced and harmonious, just as most musicians want to create scores that are rhythmical and harmonious. Indeed, the idea of harmony is a key desire in all the arts, and the fundamental dividing line between the order of art on one side, and the chaos of life on the other. The problem with this desire, for both visual artists and musicians, is that too much harmony leads to dull, predictable and repetitive work, and so the solution is, as Stass taught his students, to introduce a visual or compositional element that cuts across the balance and harmony. This gives a work of art an unexpected quality, or an element of surprise, that keeps the viewer interested.

In this I think we have a useful introduction to Stass's paintings and sculptures, which we can apply when looking at his work in a gallery or book illustration. Alongside repetitions of colour, shape and line which create harmonious rhythms in his paintings, we can see where he has cut across those rhythms by introducing an unexpected colour or shape that piques our interest by threatening to undermine the harmony of the image. The trick in art is to pique that interest in the viewer without wholly undermining the harmony of the image. This is what Stass meant by the word 'tension'. Art was always, in his view, a combination of rhythm and tension, and these two words would often punctuate his conversations on art.

This sophisticated understanding of art was, for Stass, ultimately derived from reading books by his hero, the art theorist Herbert Read. But it is particularly remarkable when we realise that Stass did not come from an educated or illustrious background. He came from what people sometimes call peasant stock. Born in the village of Anaphotia, near Larnaca, on 17 March 1933, Stass spent his youth tending his family's flock of sheep and goats in the fields around the village. Schooling was intermittent, but he attended often enough to

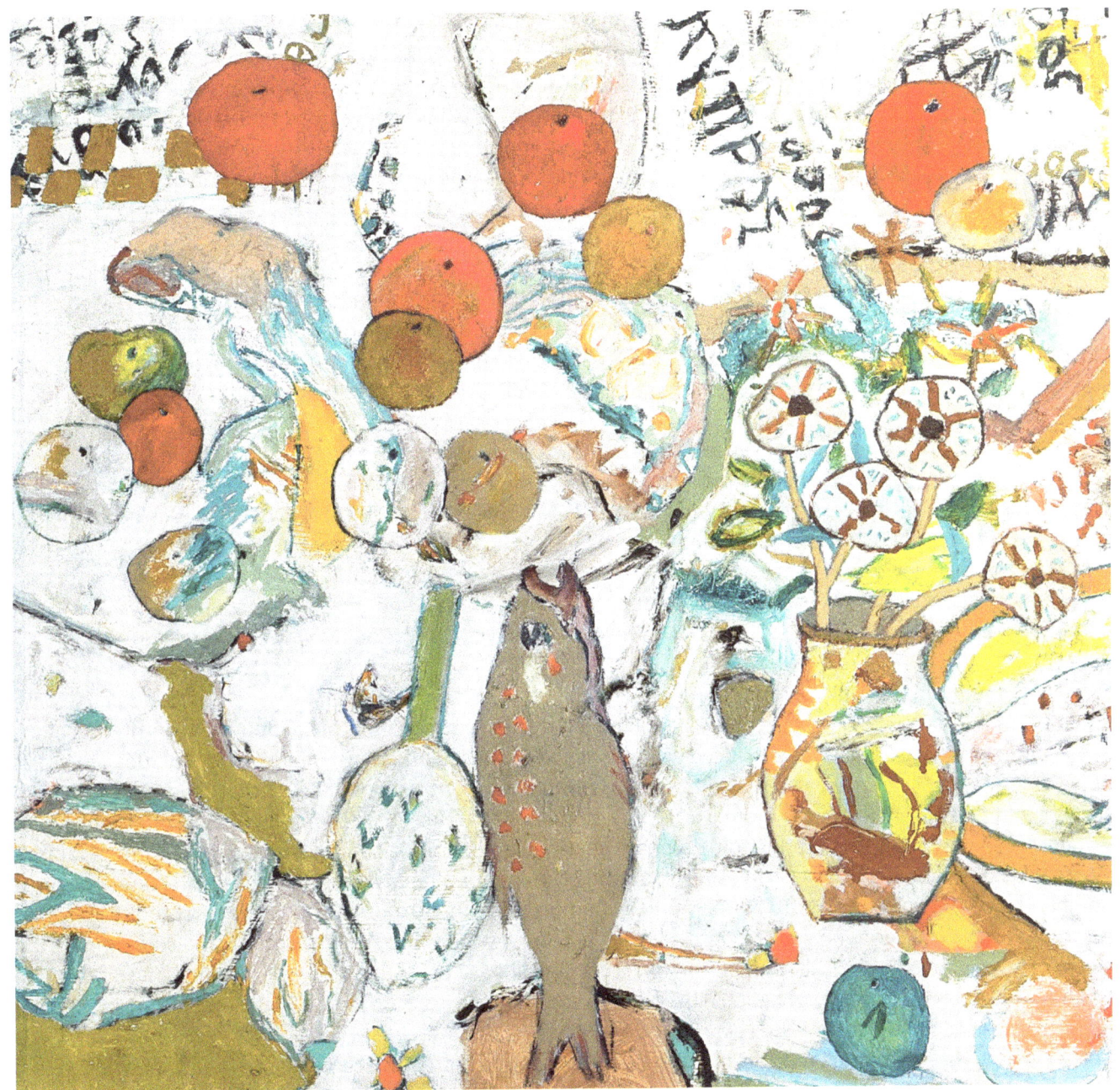

1964
Still Life with Fish

learn to read and write, and at some point he thought he could be apprenticed as a printer, working in one of the print shops of the many newspapers published in Cyprus. Stass's left-wing political sympathies would have helped this ambition as the printing industry was then dominated in Cyprus by communist trades unions, and Communist Party membership was almost obligatory for anyone wanting to gain a printing apprenticeship. But, as Stass's brother, Peter, has said, there was always something about Stass that wanted more from life. And so, in 1953, Stass left Cyprus, with just five pounds to his name, and a one way ticket to England, in search of a better life.

This was not such a surprising decision for him to make. In 1953 Cyprus was a British colony and Britain had long presented itself to its colonial subjects as the mother country. As a result, thanks to the British Nationality Act of 1948, not only was Stass classified as British, but he had the right to settle in the United Kingdom. And so, after a long overland journey across Europe, and with just one pound remaining in his pocket, Stass arrived in London and stood alone on the platform at Victoria railway station, wondering what to do next.

It is difficult to imagine the sense of fear and excitement Stass must have felt arriving in London. As far as he was aware, he knew no one in the vast city. Certainly he had nowhere to go. Yet, only a few minutes after stepping off the train, Stass experienced what he later called 'one of those strange coincidences in life.' From the other side of the ticket barrier he heard a voice calling his name. At first he thought it was a mistake, but soon he saw a familiar face. It was a man named Stelios Votsis, a fellow Cypriot already living in London as an art student. Only later did Stass discover this meeting was not a miracle at all. Worried that her son would arrive in London on his own, Stass's mother, Basilisa, had written to Votsis to say Stass was on his way.

It is tempting to date the start of Stass's interest in art to this meeting. Stass and Votsis would become lifelong friends, and certainly Votsis took Stass around many of the major sights of London, including its museums and galleries. In these Stass was introduced to some of the greatest works of art in the world. But, despite Votsis being an art student, there was no sign yet that Stass would follow in his footsteps. At that time Stass's route to success in his new homeland was more likely to be along a road travelled by so many other Cypriot emigres to Britain, namely through the catering trade. Consequently, despite visiting London's great art collections, Stass's working life at the time was as a pot-washer, cook and occasional waiter in London's cafés and restaurants, most notably the ABC Tea Room in Tottenham Court Road. It was also the restaurant trade that first took him to the north of England, to Leeds, in 1955, where another brother, Andrew, had already settled and was running the city's first Greek restaurant, called the Montevideo.[2] On the back of all things Greek becoming fashionable in Britain in the late 1950s and early 1960s, the Montevideo was a Mecca for the equally fashionable artists and art students of Leeds University and Leeds College of Art. One of those artists was the Head of Fine Art at Leeds College of Art, Harry Thubron, who decided, for reasons that appear to have remained as unfathomable to Stass as anyone else, that Stass should enrol as one of his art students.

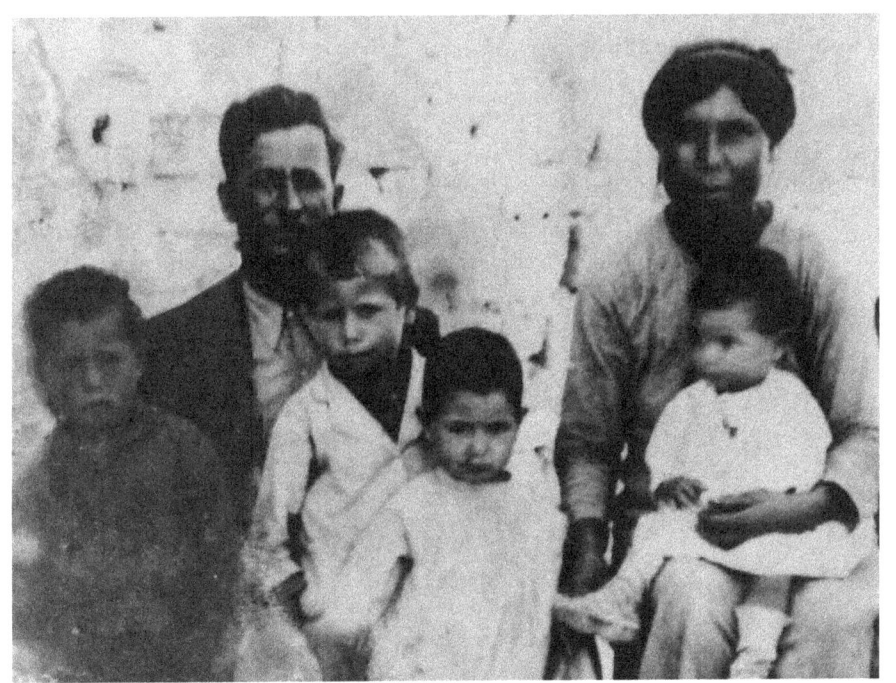

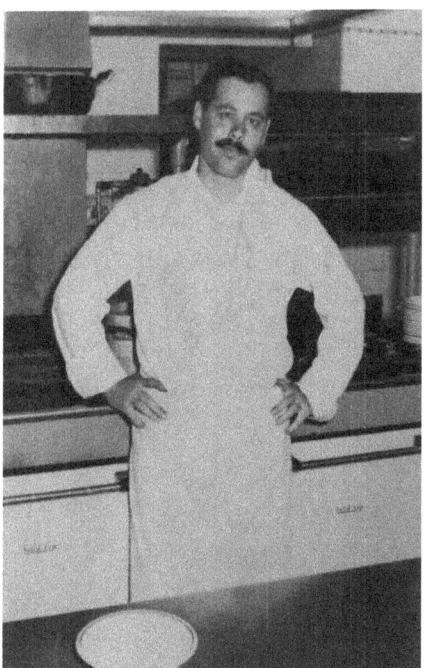

1938
Stass with his parents and brothers in Cyprus

1955
Stass Paraskos in the Montevideo Restaurant, Leeds

In making this decision Thubron had no obvious evidence to suggest Stass was a budding artist, and Stass even lacked the most basic of entrance qualifications to allow him to enrol as a student. One wonders if it was something Stass said while serving at Thubron's table, maybe a story about visiting the National Gallery or Tate in London in the company of Votsis, that led to this extraordinary decision. Or perhaps it was an idealistic belief, on the part of Thubron, that the former shepherd from Larnaca, now working in a Greek restaurant in Leeds, was another 'Giotto amongst the sheepfolds', and that his role was to play a modern-day Cimabue.[3] It seems unlikely we will ever know the truth, but it was little short of a miracle. Although the lack of any formal entrance qualifications meant Stass was never awarded a diploma or degree for his studies, as far as Thubron, the other tutors and his fellow students were concerned, Stass was as much a part of Leeds College of Art as they were. And to say Stass was overwhelmed by this change in his life would be an understatement. As he later said of Leeds College of Art, 'It was like entering paradise for me.'

By this time Stass had met the woman who would become his wife for the next half century, Mary. Mary was English, born in Staffordshire, but raised since early childhood in Leeds, and when Stass met her she was working as a photographer's assistant. They married in 1957 and their first child, christened Stass, but usually known as Stan, was born a year later. Three more children followed over the next six years, Margaret, Paul and Christopher.[4]

2. Panikos Panayi, Spicing up Britain: The Multicultural History of British Food (London: Reaktion Books, 2010) 158
3. According to the Italian Renaissance writer Giorgio Vasari the artist Cimabue discovered the young Giotto, who would go on to become one of the greatest Renaissance artists, tending sheep in the Tuscan hills. From this comes the phrase 'Giotto amongst the sheepfolds'.
4. I was born at the end of the decade, in 1969

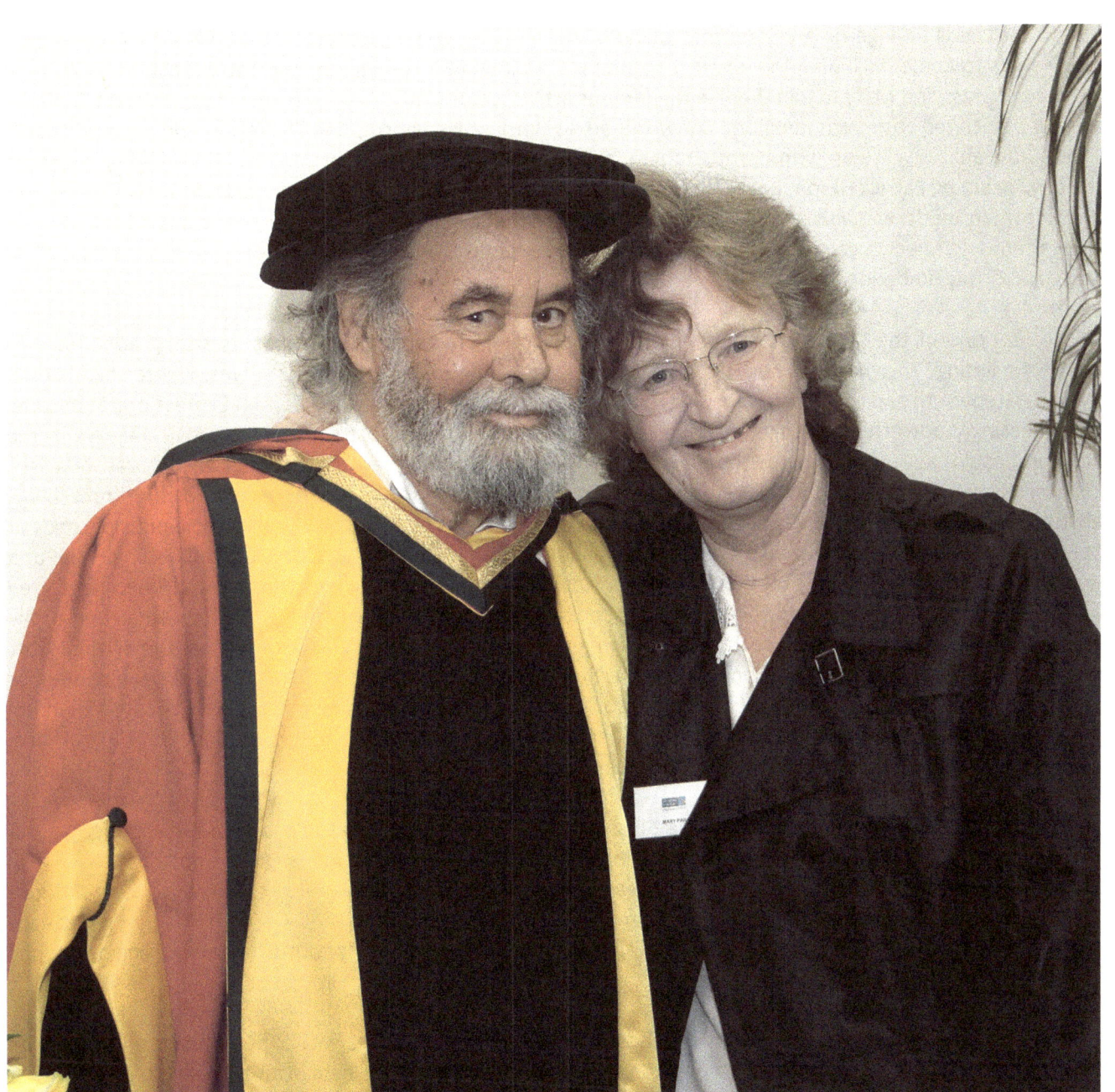

2008
Stass and Mary Paraskos at Stass's award of an honorary doctorate by the University of Bolton

At Leeds College of Art Stass met many of the people who would help shape his artistic career for many years to come, including the abstract painters Wilhelmina Barns-Graham and Terry Frost. In 1958, they persuaded Stass and Mary to join them in the famous artists' colony of St Ives, in Cornwall, south-west England, a place associated with such luminaries of world art as Barbara Hepworth, Ben Nicholson and Bernard Leach. There Stass shared a studio with Barns-Graham, and found himself in the company of other leading artists of the day, including Patrick Heron, Roger Hilton and Peter Lanyon. The art collector Ronnie Duncan, who Stass had first known in Leeds, was also a frequent visitor to Frost's studio in St Ives, and he, Terry and Stass soon became close friends. In effect, a youthful artistic community was rapidly forming along a curious Leeds-St Ives axis, and Stass was firmly embedded in it.

Yet one of the stranger features of this community in relation to Stass was its strong adherence to abstract painting. This was the most fashionable art form of the time, not only in St Ives, where the abstract legacy of Hepworth and Nicholson was still strong, but more widely as American Abstract Expressionism became an increasingly powerful influence on British art. The divide between abstract and figurative painters in the art world could be a vicious one, with real and often personal hostility between abstract and figurative artists. Yet Stass's preference for figurative painting seems never to have led to antagonism towards him from fellow abstract painters. In part this was due to Stass's personality. He was good company, and in the pubs of Leeds or St Ives he could hold an audience with funny stories about his early life in Cyprus, or his friends in England. But it was also due to Stass's painting method. Although Stass often had a narrative or story in mind when he started a painting, and he produced many overtly political paintings in which the story being told was important to the image, he never sought to illustrate those stories in a straightforward way. In fact, sometimes the original story would be forgotten during the painting process, as Stass would let the painting dictate its own development as it was being made. Consequently a figure placed in a field would ceased to be a figure and become a kind of abstract shape, or form, that might require another shape to be placed next to it to balance out the painting, even if this made no sense in terms of the story being told.

This approach to story telling made Stass's art closer in spirit to that of many of his abstract painter friends, rather than traditional figurative painting. But there are also clear passages of abstract painting in Stass's work which are easy to see in the corners and backgrounds of his images, where figurative elements give way to abstract forms. These abstract passages are legacies of Stass's working method, with his paintings usually starting as abstract compositions of colours and shapes, which only gradually became figurative as he developed them.

Yet, with a young family to support, life in the tiny village of St Ives was difficult financially, and soon Stass had to return to Leeds, after less than two years away. He continued to help in his brother's restaurant, but in 1961 Thubron offered him his first teaching work at Leeds College of Art. Further part-time work followed at Leicester College of Art (now called De Montfort University), where he befriended another Leeds-based artist,

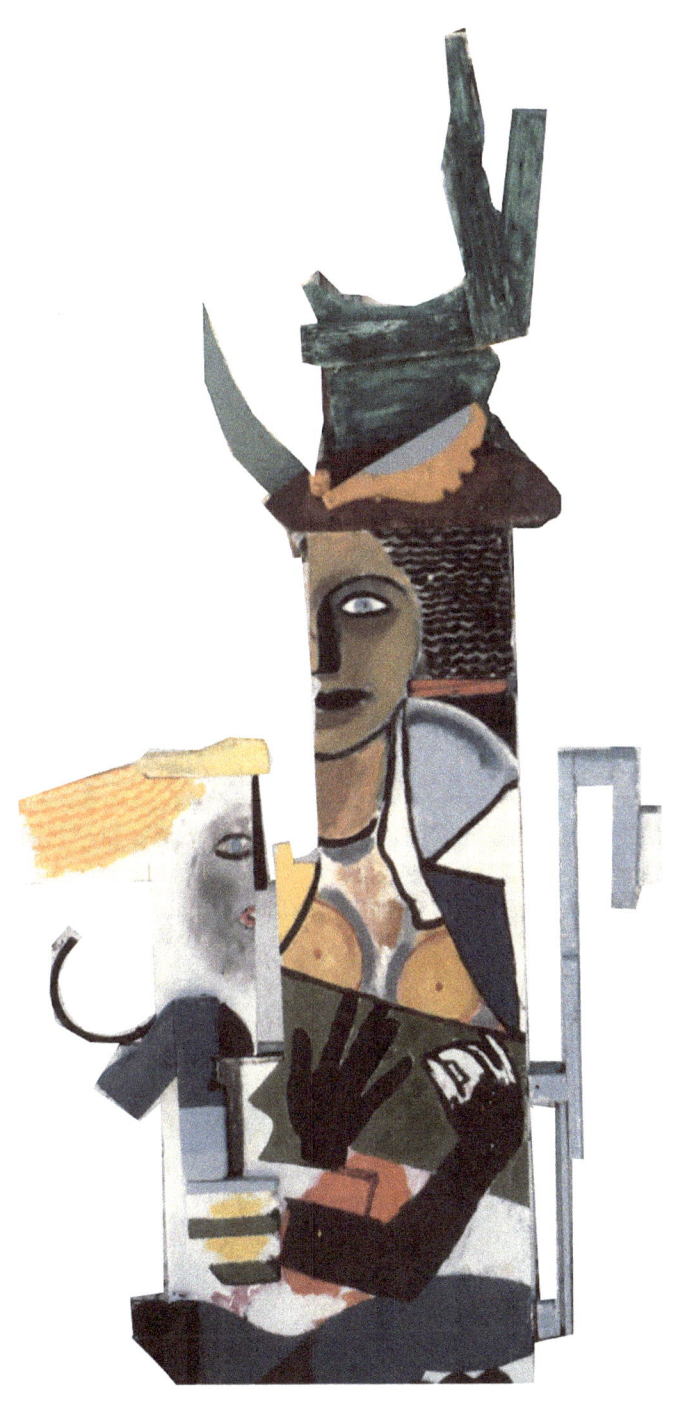

1988
The Black Glove

Laurie Burt. Burt would eventually move to Cyprus and establish one of the first contemporary art galleries on the island.

As in St Ives, this second period in Leeds was a time when Stass built friendships with key figures in the British art world, not only Burt, but artists such as Dennis Creffield, Thomas Watt, Michael Sandle, Doug Sandle, Robin Page, Tom Pemberton and others, most of whom were also on the part-time teaching circuit in various art schools. The strong reputation of Leeds as a centre for radical art also brought many other cultural figures to the city, most notably those appointed to become artists and poets in residence at the University of Leeds, on its Gregory Fellowship programme. Stass was particularly drawn to the poets and he befriended Peter Redgrove, Martin Bell and others. He also became friends with budding young poets, studying at the University, most notably Tony Harrison and George Szirtes. All of these key cultural figures in Leeds would work together, often share houses, and socialise in the key pubs at the heart of the city's extraordinary cultural scene in the 1960s – the Fenton, Eldon, Cobourg and Queen Victoria.

It was at this time, in 1966, that Stass was invited by Patrick Hughes, who also taught at Leeds College of Art, to hold his first solo show in the College's gallery, called the Leeds Institute Gallery. Yet, three days after the exhibition opened on 25 April it was raided by the police and closed down. An anonymous complaint had been made that the exhibition was obscene, and Stass was charged by the police. Immediately a defence campaign was set up, co-ordinated by John Jones, a tutor at Leeds University, which resulted in people from across the art world being contacted and asked to help. Many did, with messages of support coming from leading cultural figures including Stephen Spender, Roland Penrose and Adrian Stokes, and Herbert Read, Norbert Lynton and Quentin Bell appearing as defence witnesses in court. Overnight Stass became an international cause célèbre, his story filling newspapers and art journals, and even the British Home Secretary (Minister of Interior), Roy Jenkins, sending a message of support via his personal private secretary, Tom Driberg. Despite all this, the case was lost. Stass was fined £20, and his offending paintings banned from public display ever again.[5]

The experience of the prosecution was undoubtedly frightening for Stass, but he was also angry. Over the next few months Stass he articles and letters in the British press accusing the authorities of turning him into a pornographer by labelling him as one.[6] After a while the anger turned into a sense of resignation, as Stass realised he would be forever associated with the obscenity trial, to the point where he sometimes wondered if it overshadowed appreciation of his later work. The events of 1966 became a story he sometimes discussed with friends over drinks, but Stass tended to downplay it when talking to journalists or art critics. Only after 2002, when the Tate gallery in London acquired two of the offending images for its collection, both oil sketches, did Stass seem to welcome people discussing this episode in his history. He realised, at last, that it was not only an important episode in his own life, but in the history of British art. He was, after all, the last artist to be successfully prosecuted by the police under an archaic law, which had previously been used against DH Lawrence.

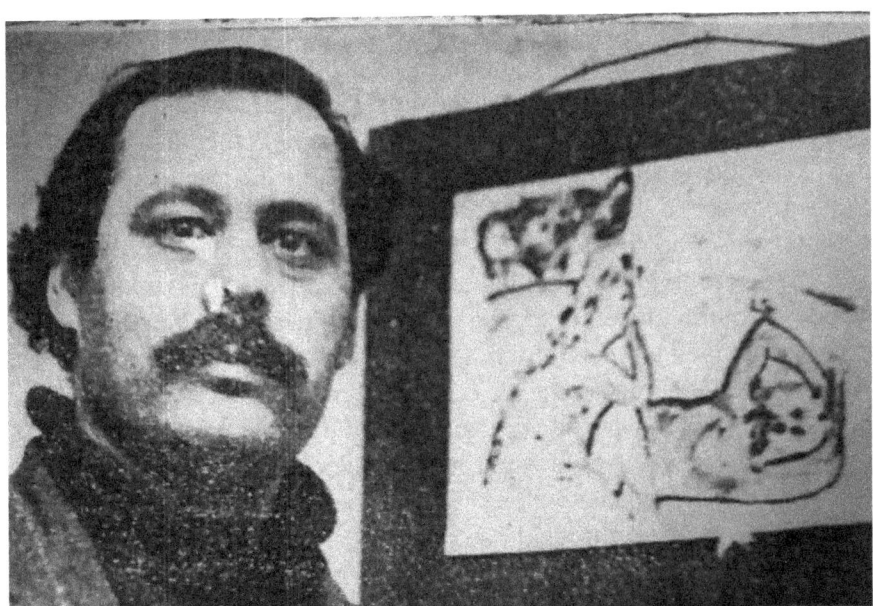

R. STASSINOS PARASKOS, two of whose pictures have been seized by the police from an ex[...] Leeds, at home in the city last night. On the wall hangs one of his paintings, in the sty[...] pictures on exhibition. (A Yorkshire Post picture.)

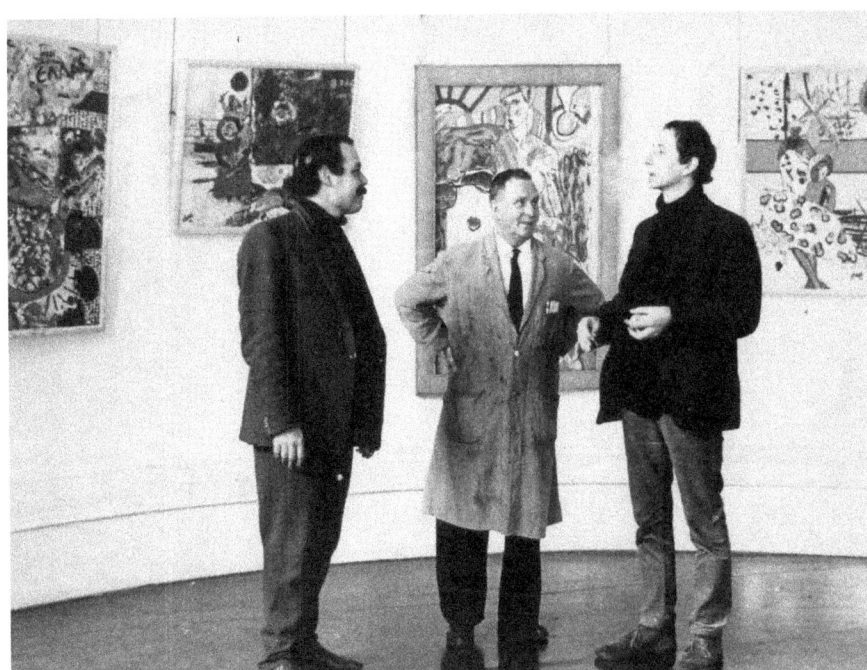

1966
Photograph Stass Paraskos in Leeds

1966
[S]tass Paraskos and Dennis Creffield at the exhibition
[L]overs and Romances', Leeds Institute Gallery, Leeds

There were also immediate benefits that stemmed from the prosecution of Stass in 1966. Offers for him to teach at the increasingly radicalised art schools across Britain started to flood in, including an invitation to spend a few days with students at the most radical art school of them all, Hornsey School of Art (now Middlesex University). Stass was also invited in 1967 to exhibit with Ian Dury at the prestigious Institute of Contemporary Arts, in London, usually known by its initials as the ICA. Yet, perhaps the most significant offer of teaching work came from an old friend, Tom Hudson. Hudson had been one of Stass's tutors as Leeds College of Art, but by 1966 he was working at Cardiff School of Art (now called Cardiff Metropolitan University). One of Hudson's jobs there was to find interesting tutors to teach at the annual Barry Summer School. This was a unique event designed to bring together teachers of art from across Britain to share new ideas and practises. By the 1960s it had developed a reputation as a centre for avant-garde practice, and was undoubtedly a key source for the spread of avant-garde artistic ideas in Britain, including practises such as performance, multimedia and overtly political art. Hudson invited Stass to teach on the Summer School alongside Terry Setch, and the effect on Stass was transformative. Returning to Leeds he quickly developed an idea to start a similar summer school in Cyprus. From the beginning he intended this to be the seed from which a Cyprus college of art would grow, making the Cyprus College of Art the legitimate offspring of Leeds College of Art and Barry Summer School.

5. Alan Travis, Bound and Gagged (London, Profile Books, 2000) 202
6. For example see Stats Paraskos, 'The Artist and the Censor' in The Leicester Mercury, 18 April 1967.

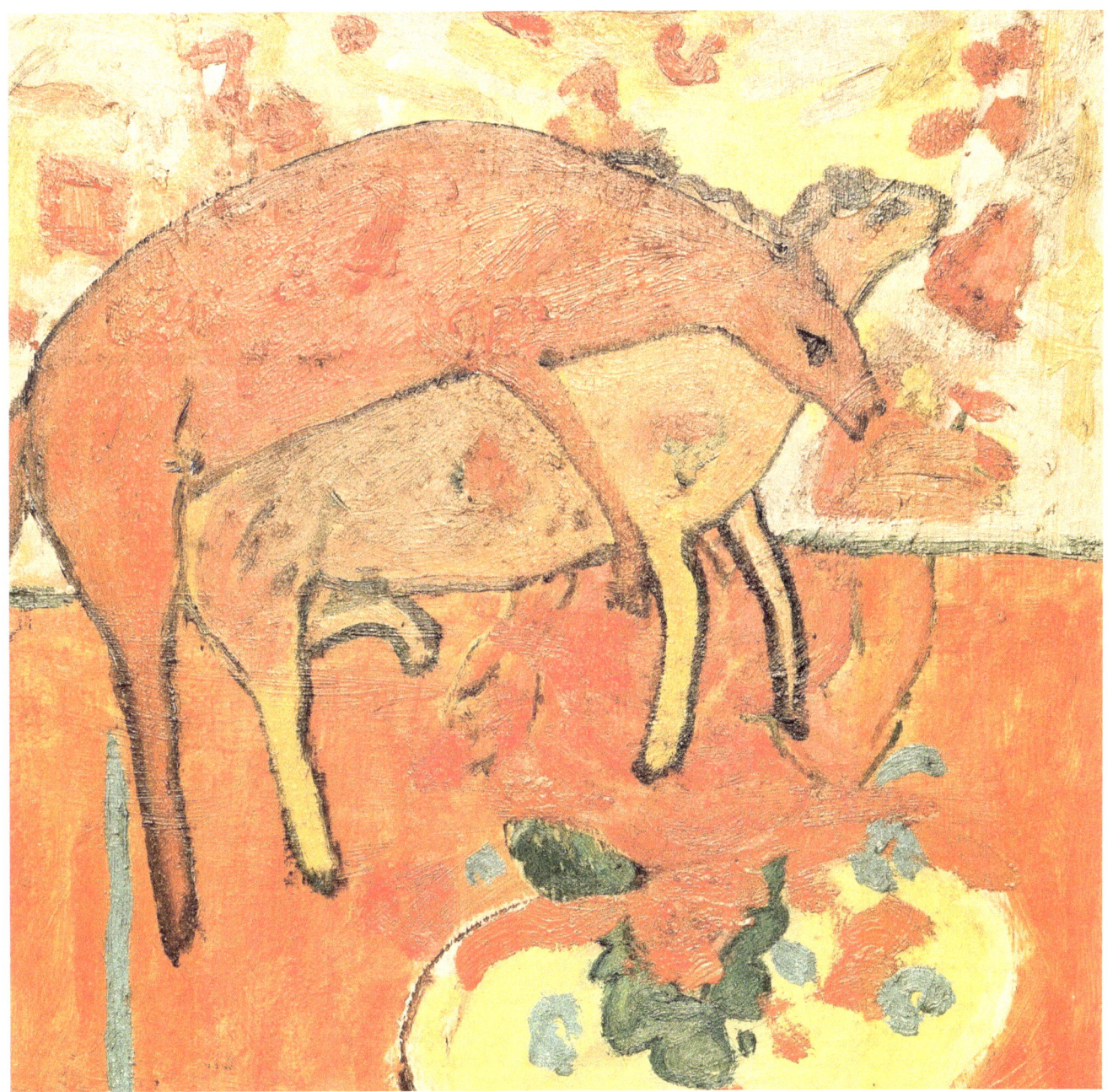

1966
Lovers and Romances I

However, Stass was never an artist who earned a great deal of money and, as we have heard, he did not come from a wealthy background. Consequently the idea of starting an art school, even in Cyprus, was either an act of astonishing idealism or extreme madness, depending on one's point of view. Nonetheless, in 1968 Stass travelled to Cyprus with Mary and their children, and the Leeds poet Martin Bell, to try and organise a Cyprus art summer school for the following year. In Stass's mind, if they could just arrange a meeting with the President of Cyprus, Archbishop Makarios, Stass would be able to tell him what a good idea an art college in Cyprus would be, and Makarios would, of course, help. Yet, as Stass's diary for that year shows, the path to seeing Makarios was far from clear. Despite being a small island, in which it is said everyone knows each other, Stass had no connections in the government. Although wealthy people can easily get to see government ministers, and even presidents, it is not so easy for a poor peasant who had emigrated to England to become a pot washer and cook. Even less easy for an artist who had caused a scandal by showing obscene paintings, and who now had a criminal record. The hope of seeing Makarios, and starting the first art college in Cyprus, seemed impossible.

But Stass faced another problem on that trip: Martin Bell. Bell was a notorious alcoholic, and during that summer he managed to scandalise the Cypriot people with his heavy drinking, to the point where his behaviour was even noticed by the island's newspapers.

One journalist wrote:

With Mr Paraskos is Mr Martin Bell, a poet who is writing a book on Cyprus, going around the streets dressed like a tramp, even though he is said to be a university lecturer – a sign of our times![7]

Bell's drunken antics, and a lack of connections in the government, seemed to doom the adventure from the start. But, in another of those 'strange coincidences in life', Stass managed to befriend a young Cypriot architect called Pefkios Georgiades, who was working on a major government contract to build dozens of primary and secondary schools across the newly independent Republic of Cyprus. Through friends of friends within government, a meeting with Makarios was finally arranged. Yet, the result of it was not quite the wholehearted support Stass had hoped for. There was no offer to build a new art school, but Makarios helped ensure that a primary school building in Famagusta would be made available to Stass during its summer holidays the following year. It was agreed two of the classrooms could be used as dormitory accommodation, one for men and one for women, and another would be provided for the students to paint in. It was a small start, but in the summer of 1969 Stass arrived in Famagusta with a group of British art students, most from Leeds, and the first Cyprus Summer School took place. The experiment was repeated for each of the following summers, with only a brief hiatus after the war in 1974, until 1978 when a full-time winter course was started. The Cyprus Summer School was renamed the Cyprus College of Art, and Stass became its Principal. Against all odds, the penniless peasant from Anaphotia had managed to found the first art school in Cyprus.

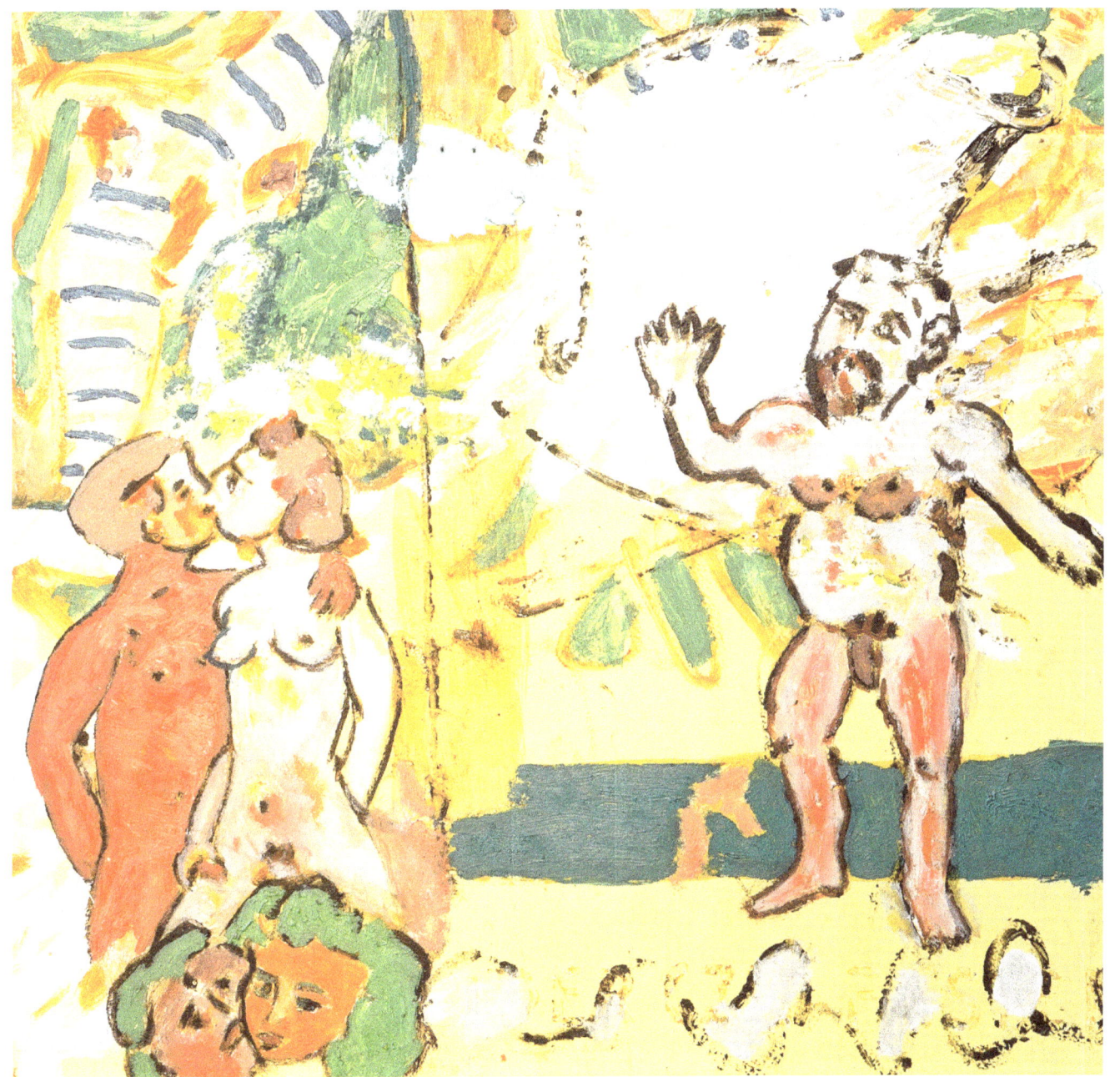

1966
Lovers and Romances IV

Despite its ongoing financial poverty, the prestige of this strange new art school was apparent very early on. Stass was able to use the friendships he had made in Britain to attract some of the biggest names in world art to Cyprus, from Terry Frost and Euan Uglow, to Rachel Whiteread and Anthony Caro. Very quickly the Cyprus Summer School, and later the Cyprus College of Art, was established on the international art circuit as one of the places artists wanted to visit, despite its studios and accommodation being so primitive. Indeed, that primitivism soon became a unique selling point for the College, as it promised artists a kind of innocent freedom in an increasingly corrupted world. But, most of all, artists came to the Cyprus College of Art because it reflected the personality of Stass.

Inevitably the stream of distinguished international visitors was also noticed by government officials in Nicosia, so that it was regularly announced to the press, throughout the 1970s and 1980s, by presidents and ministers alike, that Stass's Cyprus College of Art would one day become the Faculty of Fine Art at the future University of Cyprus, with Stass as the first Professor of Fine Art. Yet when the University of Cyprus was founded in 1989 this never happened. Stass had his own beliefs as to why the government went back on its promises, which it would be inappropriate to discuss here. But it filled him with a profound sense of betrayal and disappointment, not least because in that same year he had taken early retirement from his university job in England, at the University for Creative Arts in Canterbury, and returned to live in Cyprus.

7. From Stass's diary entry for 7 September 1968, reproduced in Michael Paraskos, In Search of Sixpence (London: Friction Fiction, 2016) p.145

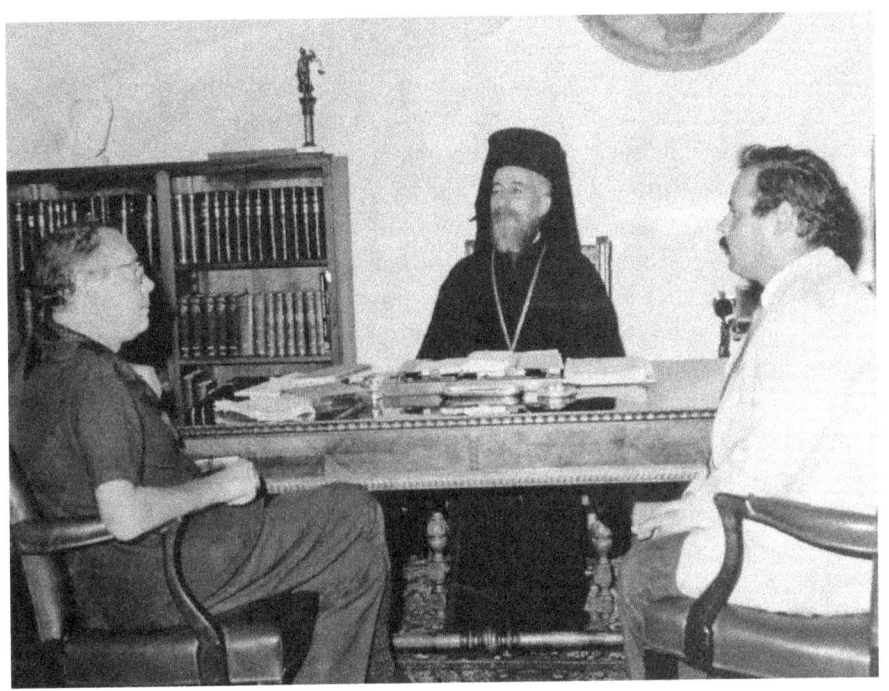

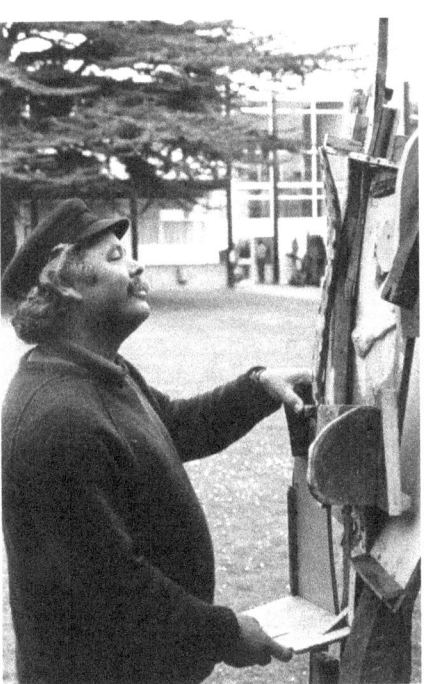

1968
Stass Paraskos and the poet Martin Bell meeting President Archbishop Makarios

1981
Stass Paraskos at Canterbury College of Art (University for Creative Arts Archive)

Stass had been teaching in Canterbury since 1970, when the University was known as Canterbury College of Art. Still living in Leeds at the time, he had been tempted down to Canterbury by another of his former tutors at Leeds College of Art, Thomas Watt. Watt had been made Head of Fine Art at Canterbury, and one of the first tasks he set himself was to bring in key people from Leeds to try and shake up the underdeveloped art teaching he found in Canterbury.[8] Consequently Stass was put to work in the painting studios, while another friend from Leeds, Tom Pemberton, went into the sculpture department. Yet this the early experience of working in Canterbury was not a happy one for Stass, and in letters written to Mary, who remained in Leeds with their children, he complained about the other tutors and the unresponsive students. After Leeds College of Art, Canterbury seemed like a backwater. It was only gradually, when Mary and the children also moved to Canterbury, and Watts's reforms started to bear fruit, that Stass's attitude to his new home and its art college changed.

Throughout this time Stass was also running his new college in Cyprus, but at a distance from England. He would visit the island during the summer months to look after the Summer School, but for the first few years students on the the newly established Postgraduate Diploma in Fine Art course at the Cyprus College of Art were expected to look after themselves. In this they were supported by short visits from artists such as Terry Frost, Jennifer Harding, Euan Uglow, Mali Morris, Jennifer Durrant, Michael Kidner, Geoff Rigden and others, but the course was designed to be as much an artist residency programme as a formal academic course. Later, in the early-1980s, when she had finished her fine art studies at Brighton University, Stass asked his daughter, Margaret, to look after the winter programme in Cyprus. And later still, in the mid-1980s, Margaret was joined by Stass's eldest son, Stanley, before Stass himself returned to Cyprus in 1989.

In spite of his disappointment at being snubbed by the University of Cyprus, there is no doubt in my mind Stass's art benefitted from his new found freedom from the stifling strictures of academic life. He was able to approach his art with renewed vigour. Although he had never stopped painting throughout his teaching career, after returning to Cyprus he was able to develop his personal visual language in new ways, not only in his paintings, but in three-dimensional sculptures. As well as a prolific output of paintings, often tacking controversial themes, such as the appalling treatment of women at the hands of men in Cyprus, and the Israeli invasion of nearby Lebanon, he orchestrated the creation of an astonishing sculpture garden that still surrounds the Cyprus College of Art campus, in the village of Lempa, just north of Paphos. As well as producing many of the key works in the sculpture wall, Stass oversaw the siting of other sculptural pieces made by his assistants, including Grahame Parry, and visiting artists like Anthony Heywood, Bob Stone, Eve Bennett and Chris Rutter, amongst others. Stass also represented Cyprus at the 1996 São Paulo Biennial, and in 2005 he received the Cyprus Award for Excellence in Arts and Science, the highest honour given by the Republic of Cyprus to artists and scientists. However, perhaps the award that filled Stass with most pride during this period was an Honorary Doctorate he received in 2008 for his services to art and education from the University of Bolton. This gave him his first ever university diploma, despite having spent fifty years teaching in British universities without one.

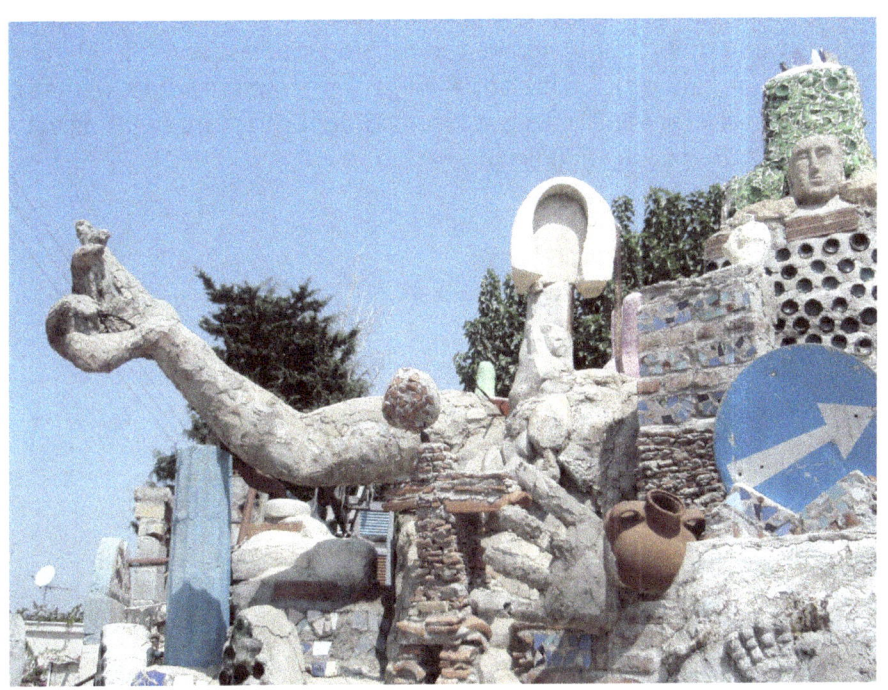
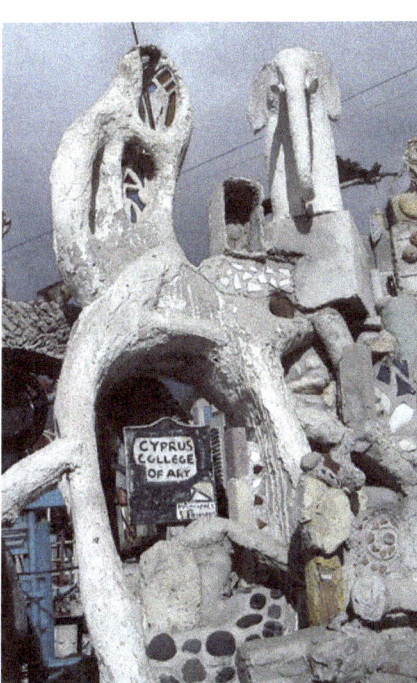

1980 - Present
Cyprus College of Art, Lemba, Paphos, Sculpture Wall

Despite illness, Stass continued to paint almost until the end of his life and he continued to teach, although in a far more informal way than anything he had done in England. Most of this took place in Paphos, where the Cyprus College of Art continued to attract artists and art students from around the world, but later he also taught in Larnaca, where a small branch of the College was opened in 2007, called the Cornaro Institute. And in 2013 Stass was also finally invited to lecture at a Cypriot university for the first and only time in his life, when the privately-owned University of Nicosia asked him to run a special project for its students.

Yet, by this time, Stass was very ill. He had suffered from diabetes for many years, and early in 2014 this caused gangrene to develop in his legs, leading to septicaemia. He died on 4 March 2014, and was buried in the village cemetery in Anaphotia, not far from the site of the house in which he was born. In many ways it was a sad and traumatic end for an artist who was well known for his vibrant zest for life. But Stass has left behind a continung legacy we can still enjoy in the form of a powerful body of paintings and sculptures. And, perhaps, most important of all, is the potent example he set every one of us of contemporary Cypriot art engaging with international culture at levels not seen on the island since the middle ages.

8. For an account of Canterbury College of Art at this time, mentioning Stass, see David Haste, The Art Schools of Kent: A Complete History (London: Werther Press, 2013) 262 and passim

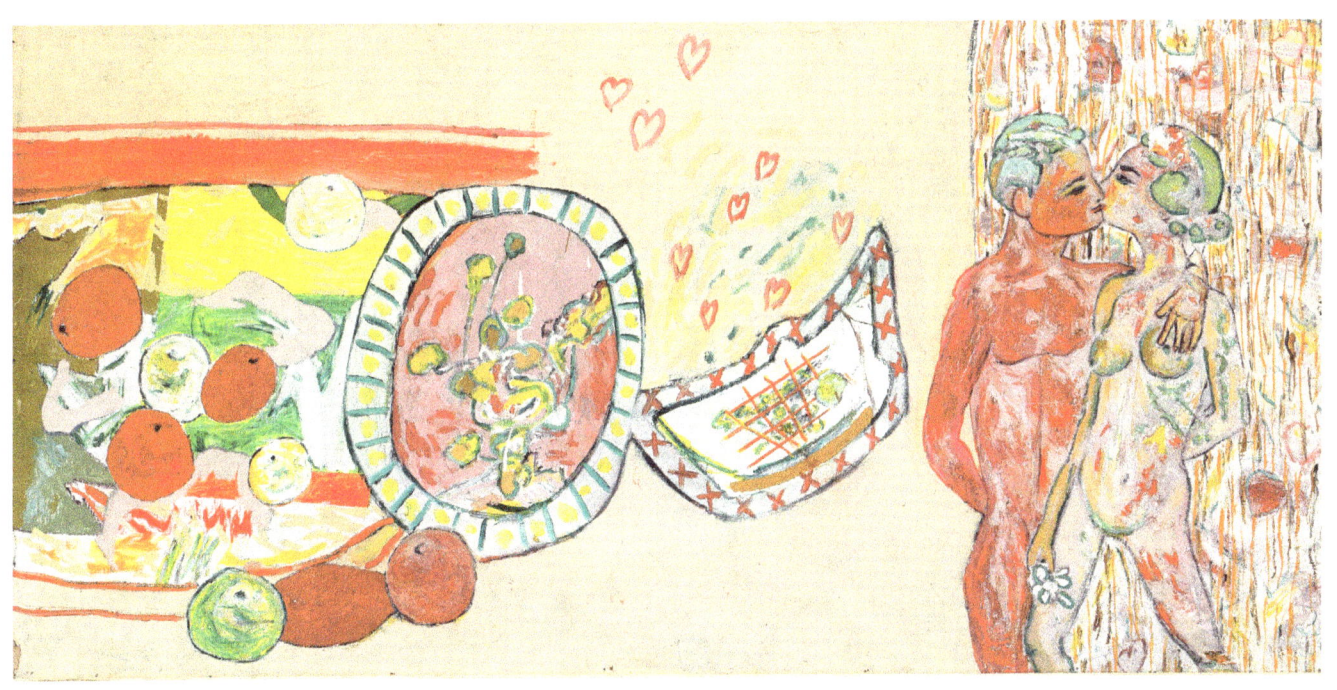

1966
The Embrace (Artemis Artform)

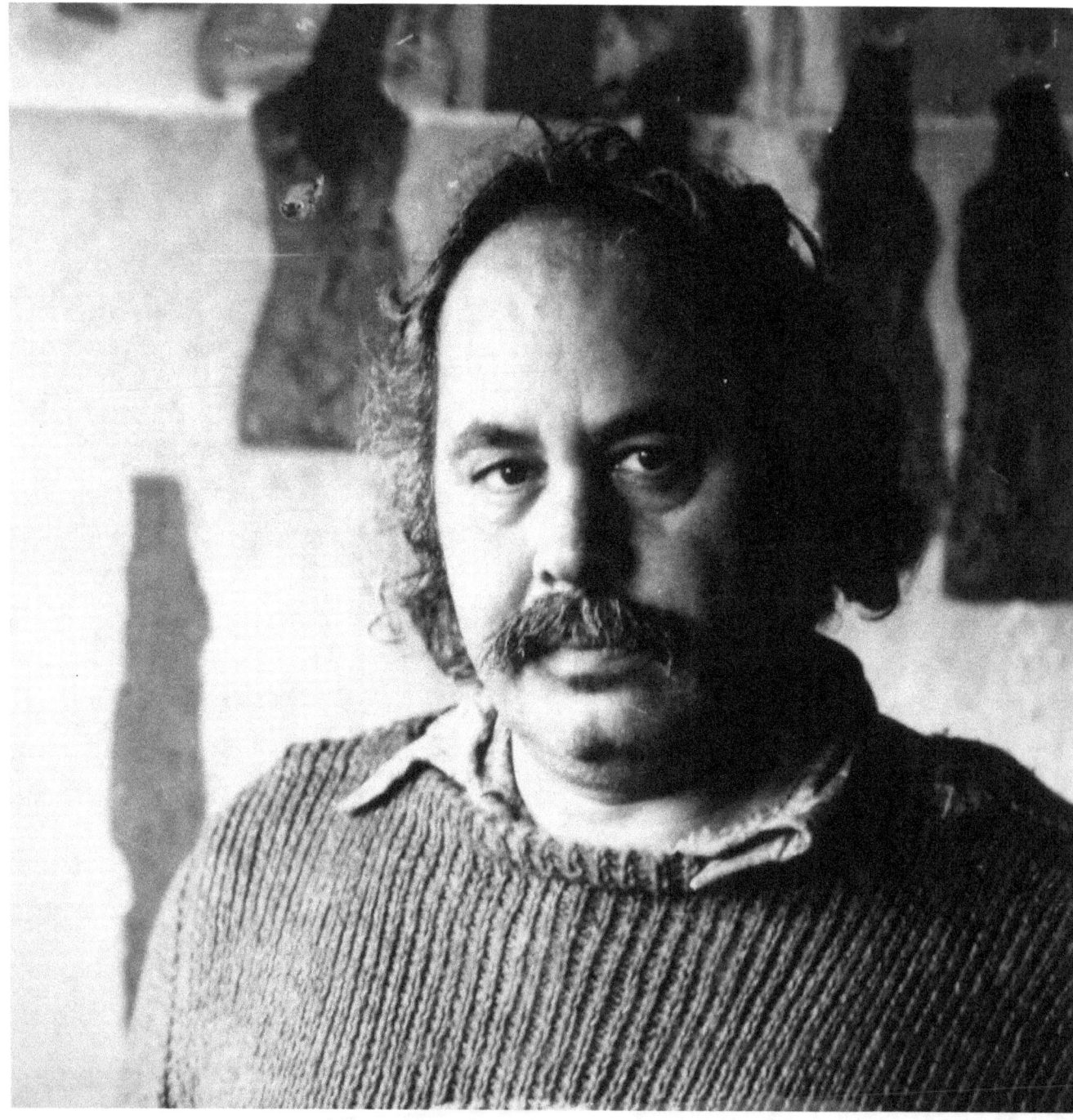

Stass Paraskos: A Celebration

Catalogue

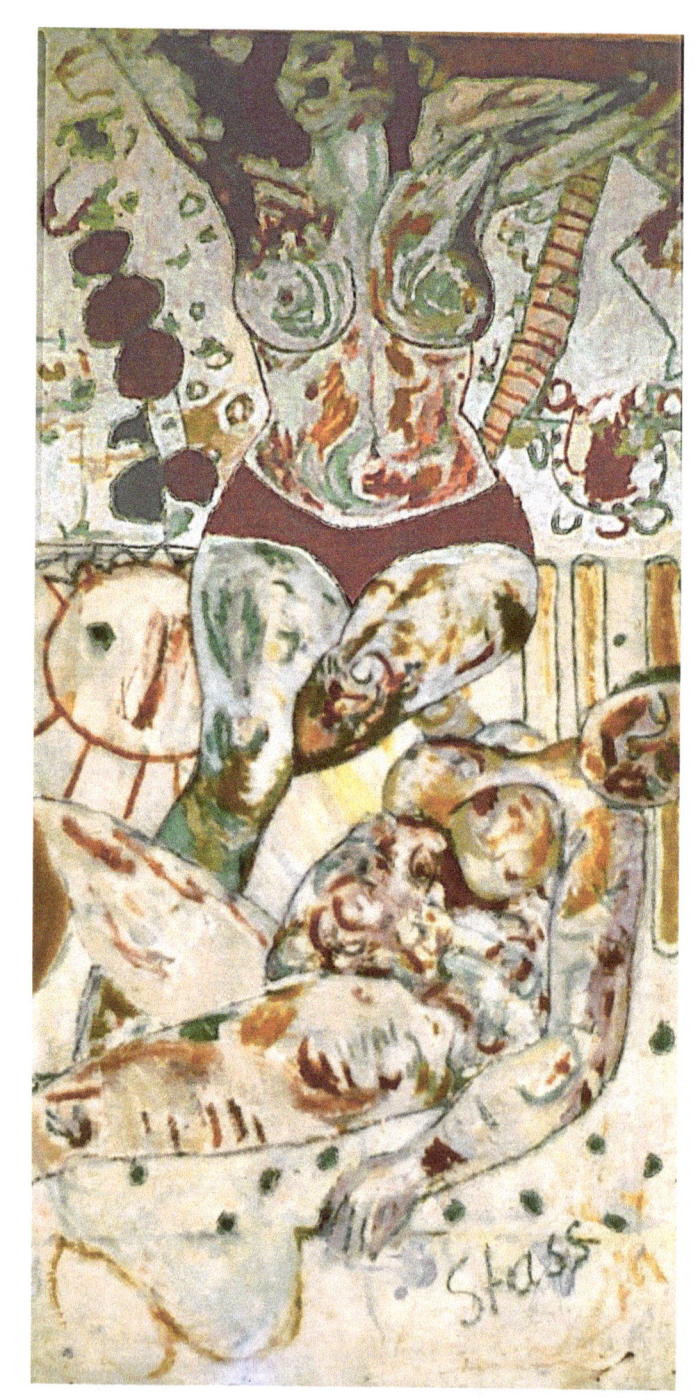

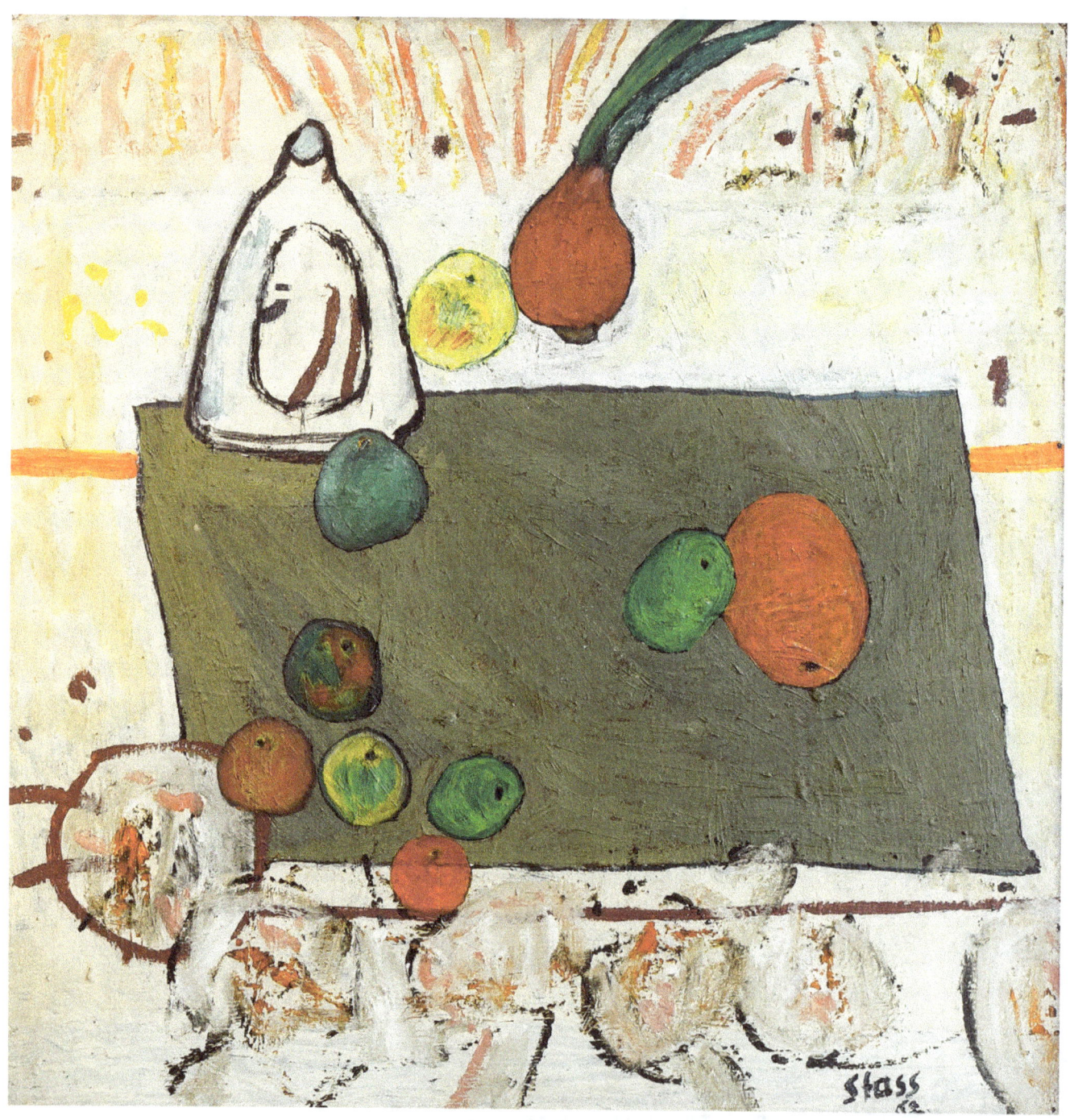

1961

Still Life with Broken Bottle

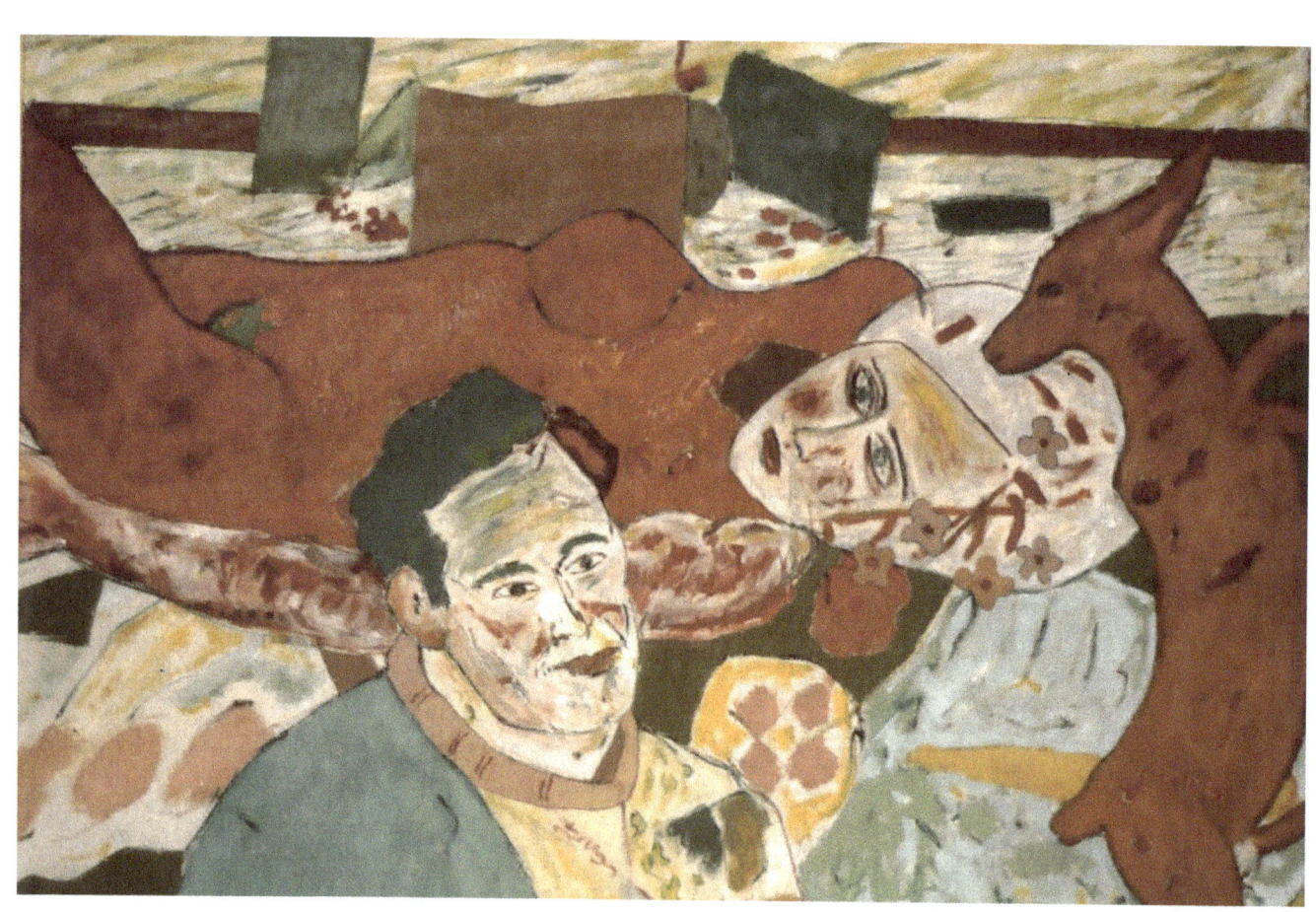

1962

The Red Fox

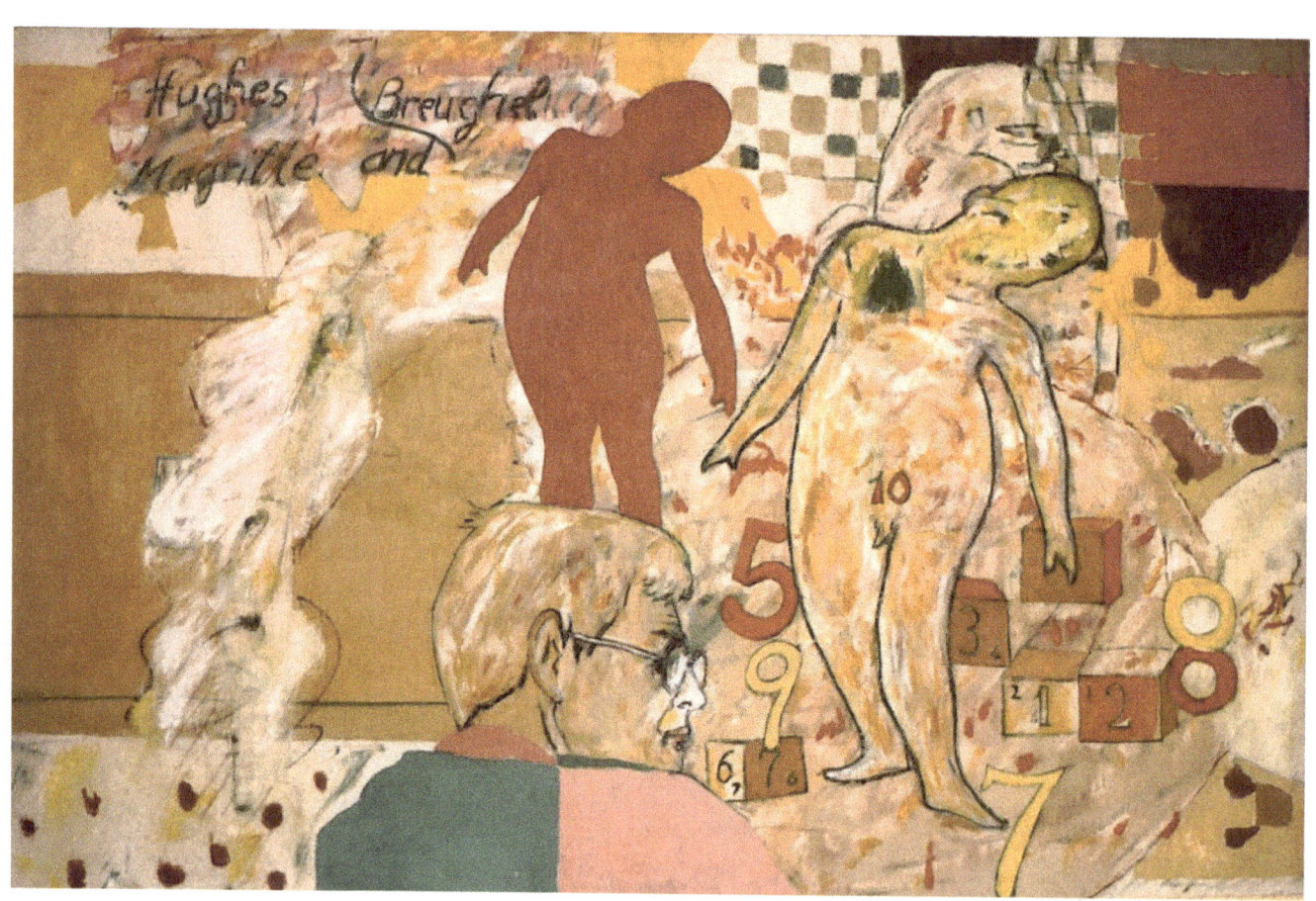

1963

Hughes, Magritte and Breughel

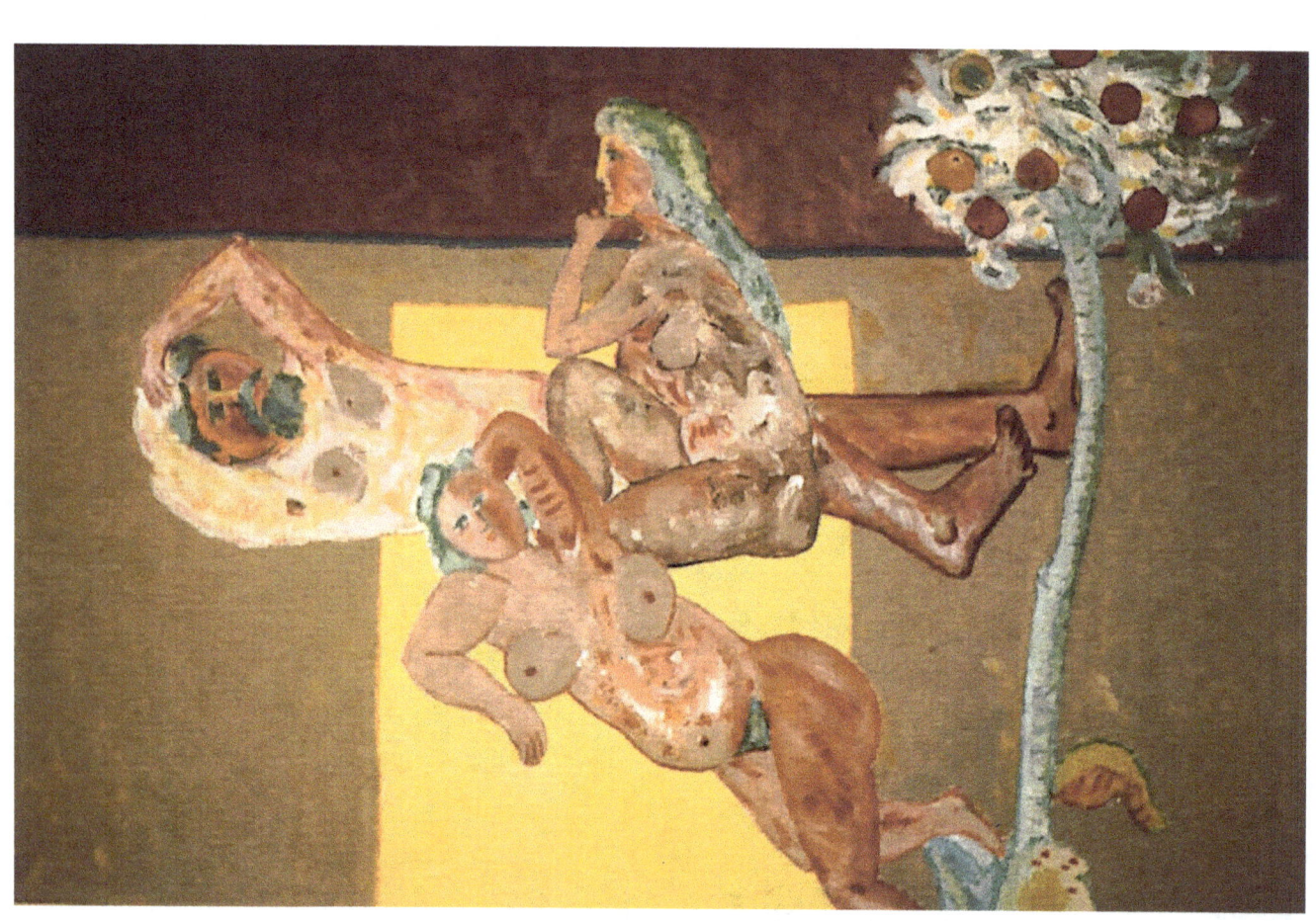

1964

Adam, Eve and Lillith

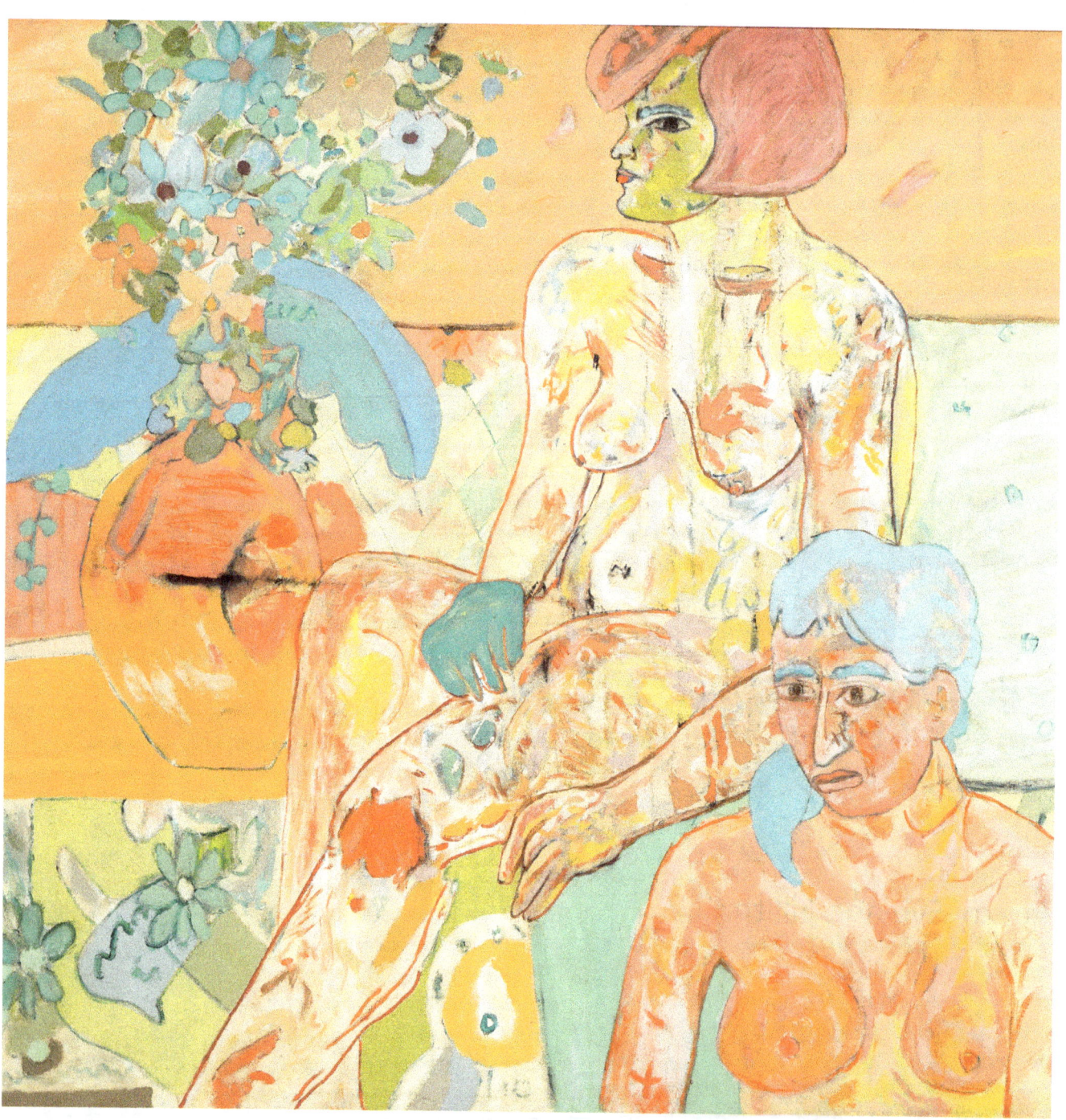

1965

Clea and Justine

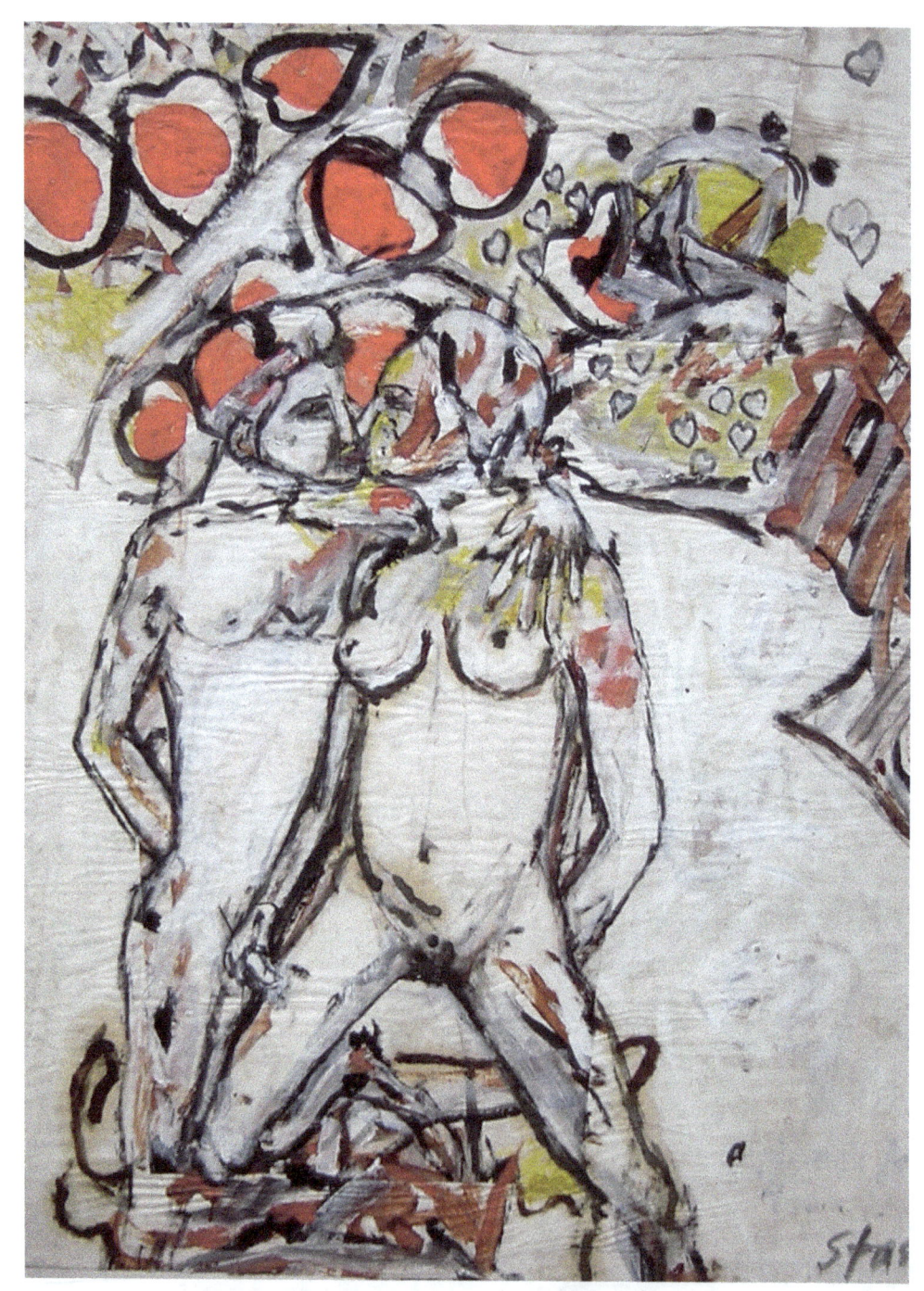

1966

Study for Lovers and Romances I (Tate Gallery, London)

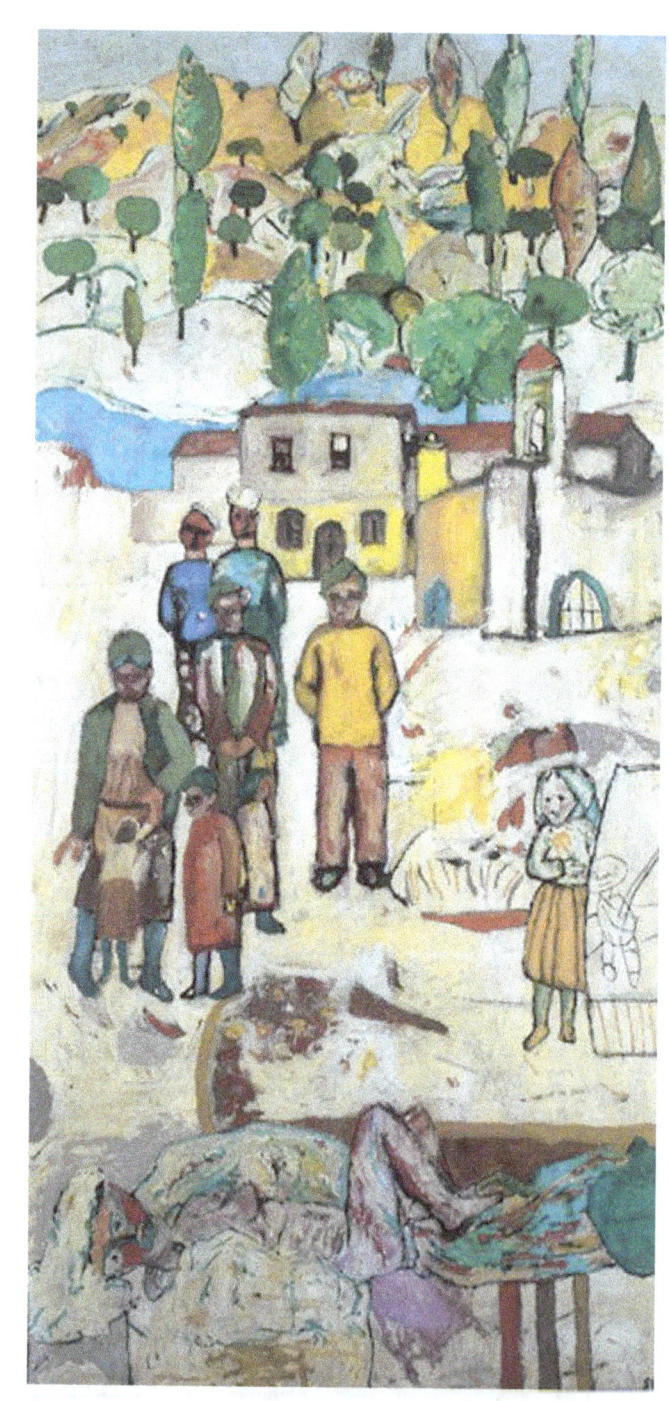

1967
Cypriot Women Raped by Turkish Soldiers
(Leeds Art Gallery Collection)

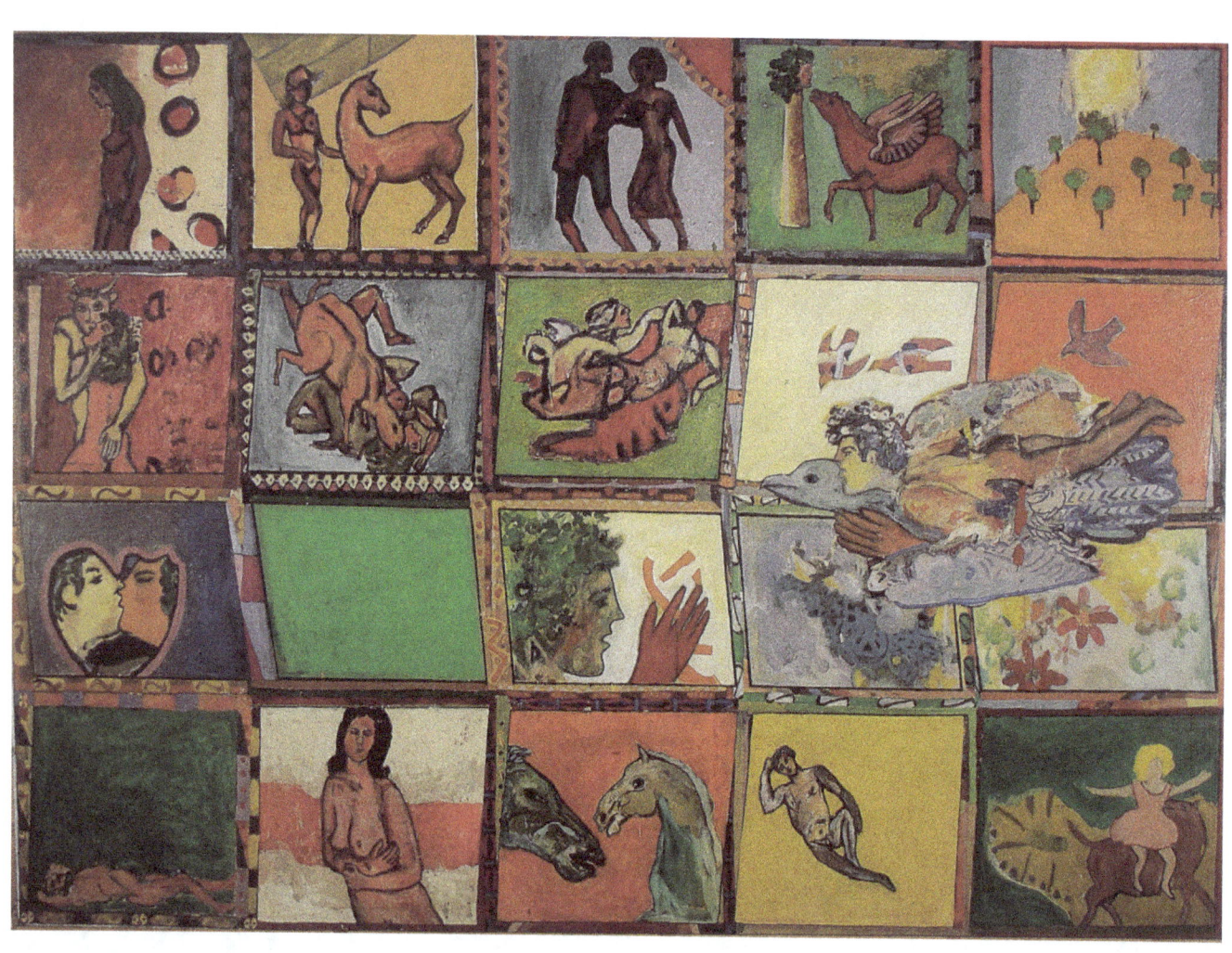

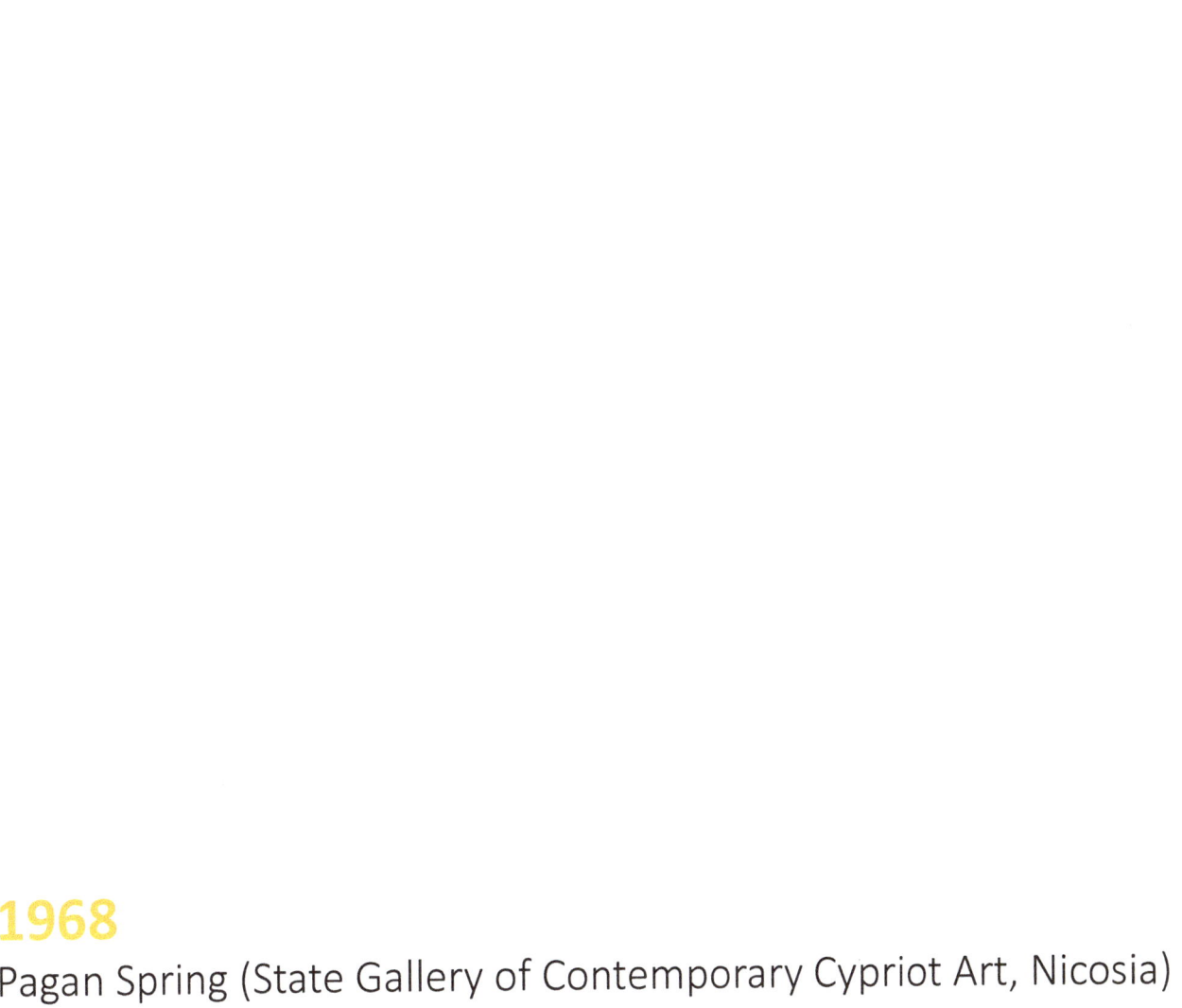

1968
Pagan Spring (State Gallery of Contemporary Cypriot Art, Nicosia)

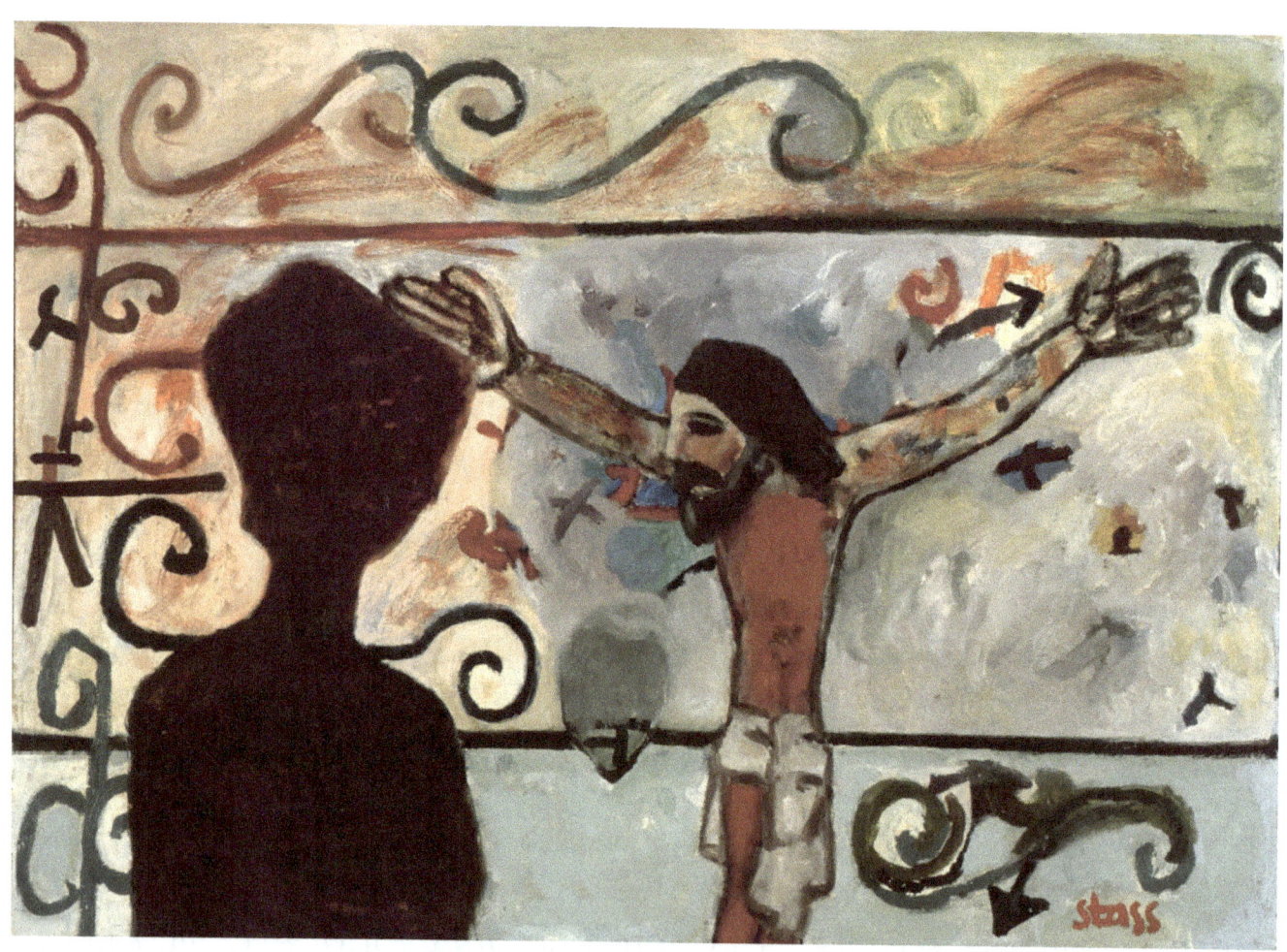

1977
Agony and Ecstasy (Archbishop Makarios III Foundation, Nicosia)

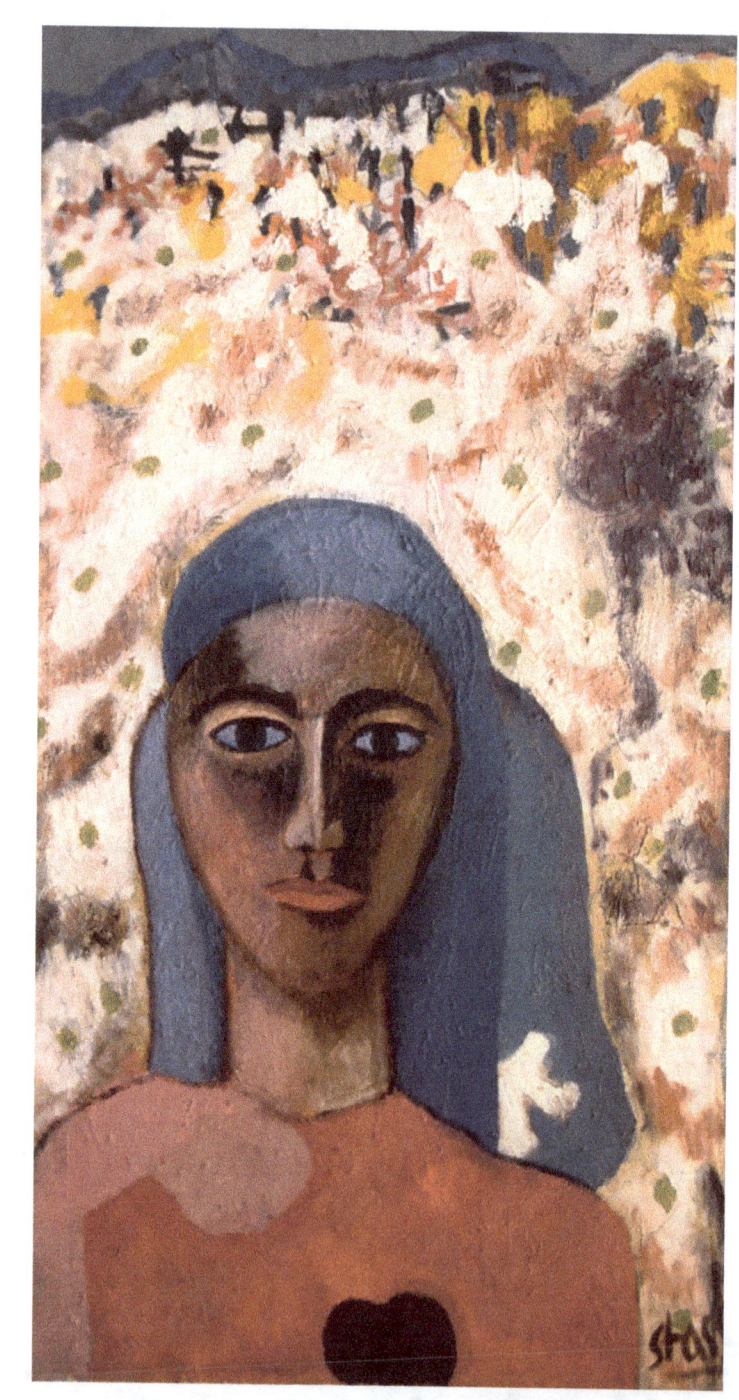

1978
Woman with Blue Hair

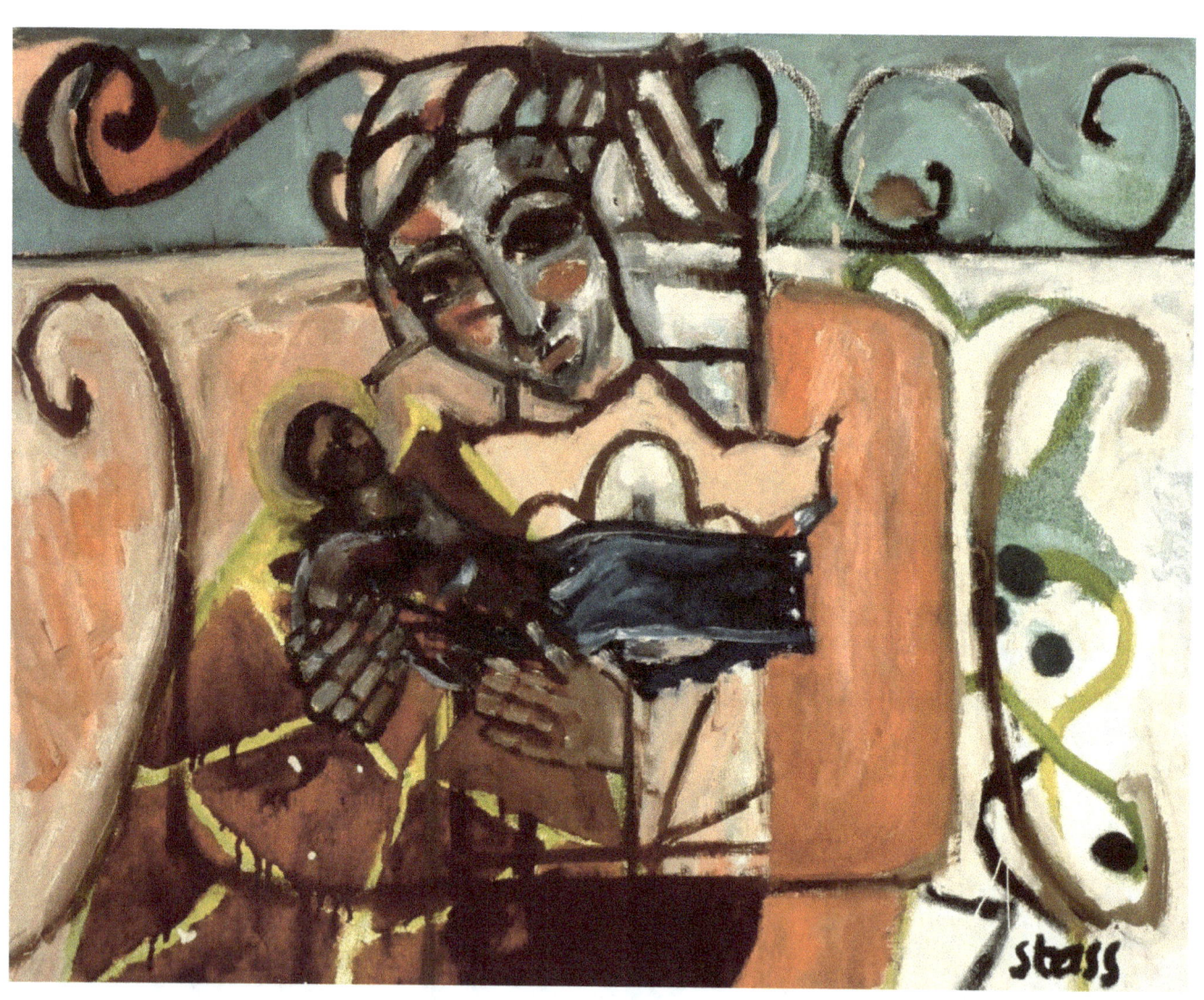

1985
Mother of God

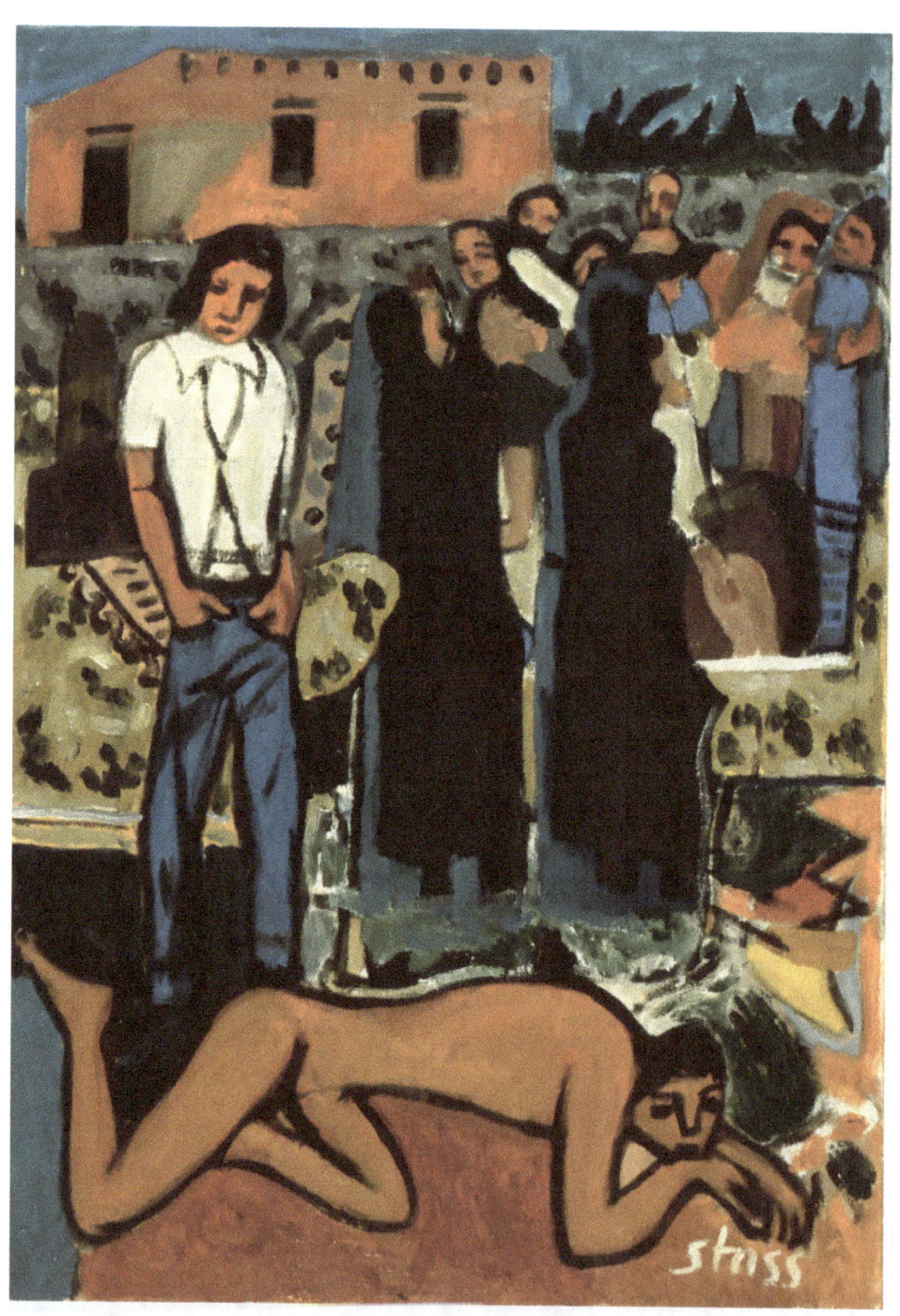

1986

The Red Nude

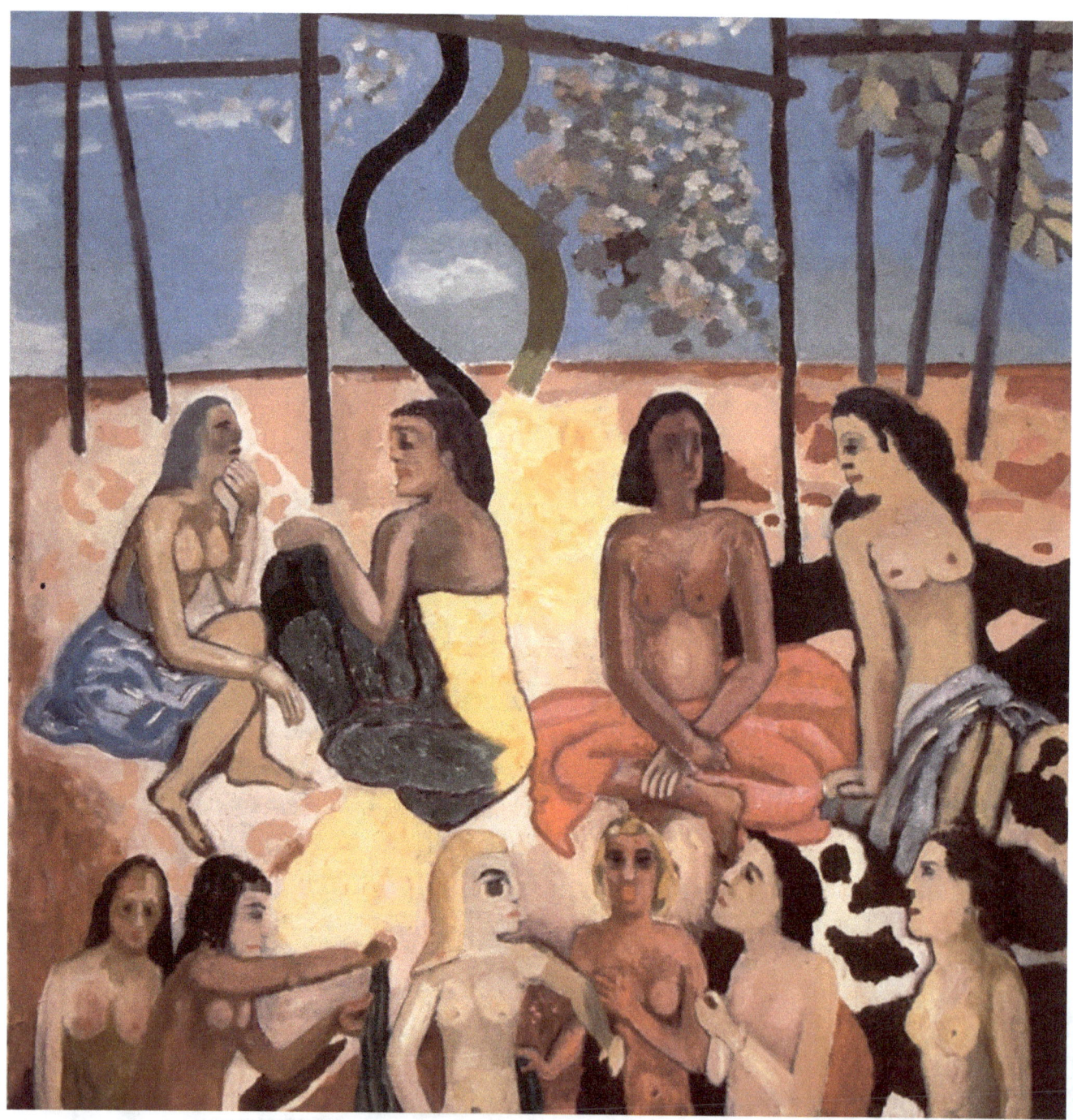

1988
Homage to Gauguin

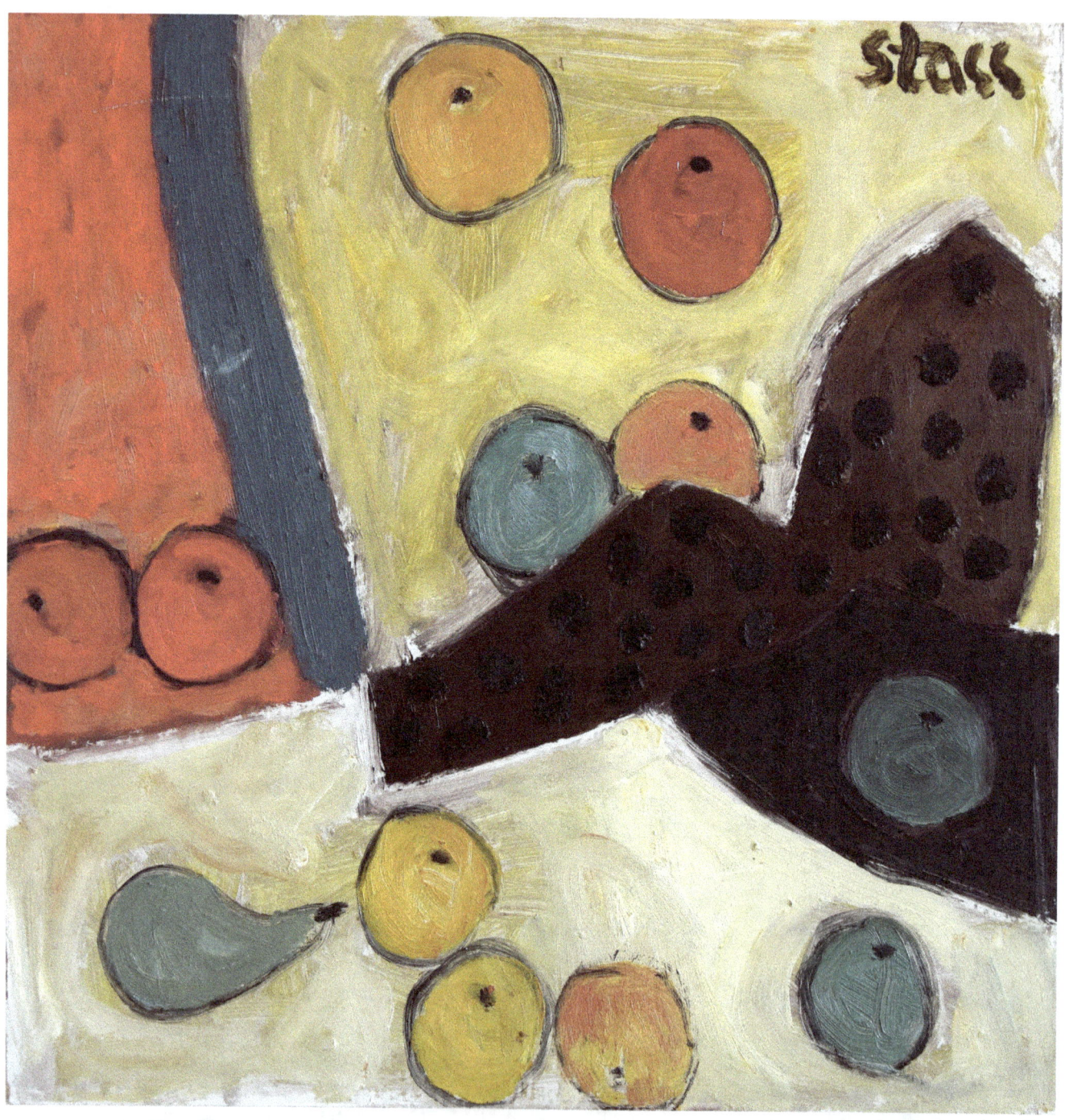

1989
Still Life with Apples, Pears and Prickly Pears

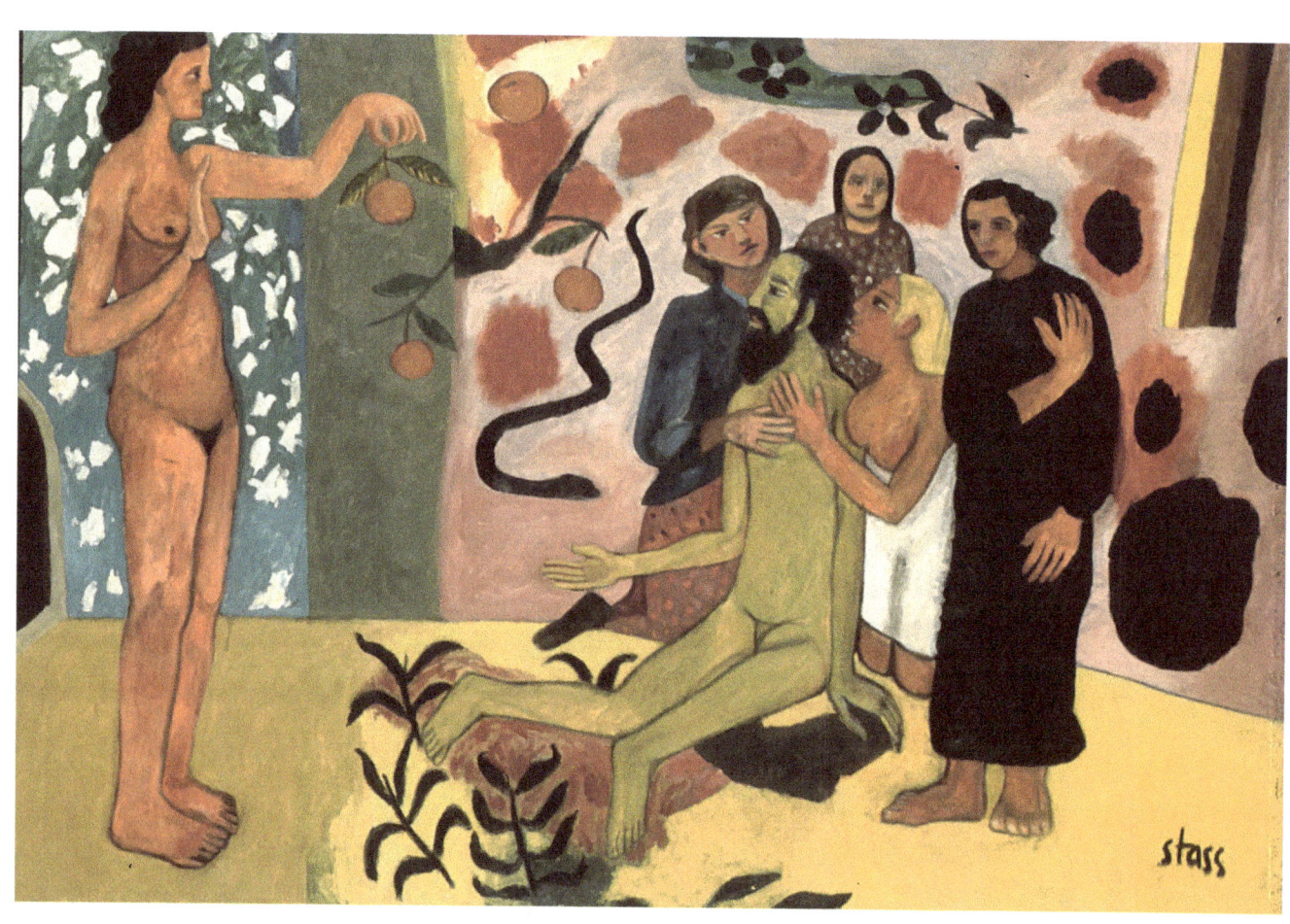

1990

St Lazarus

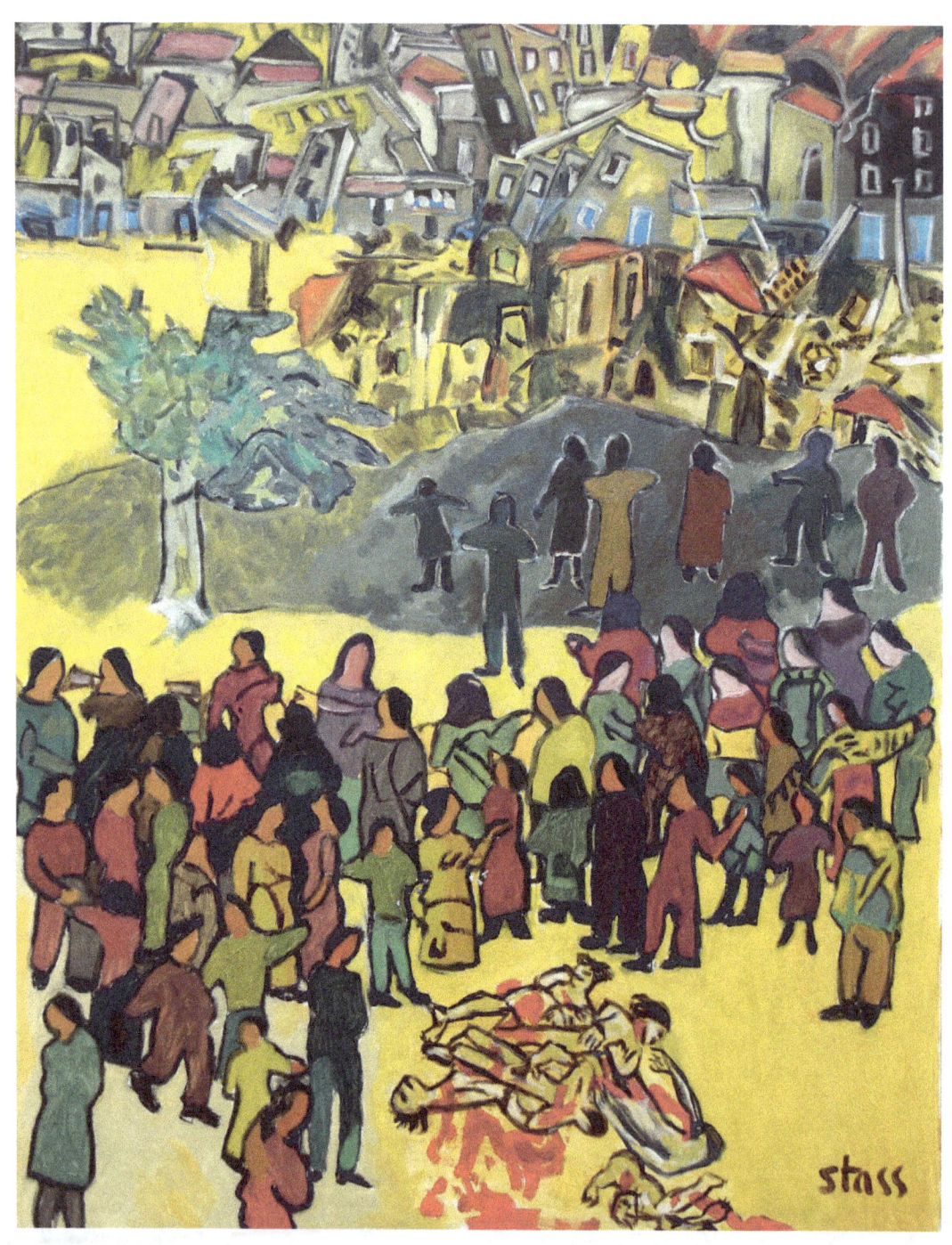

1992

Massacre at Qana

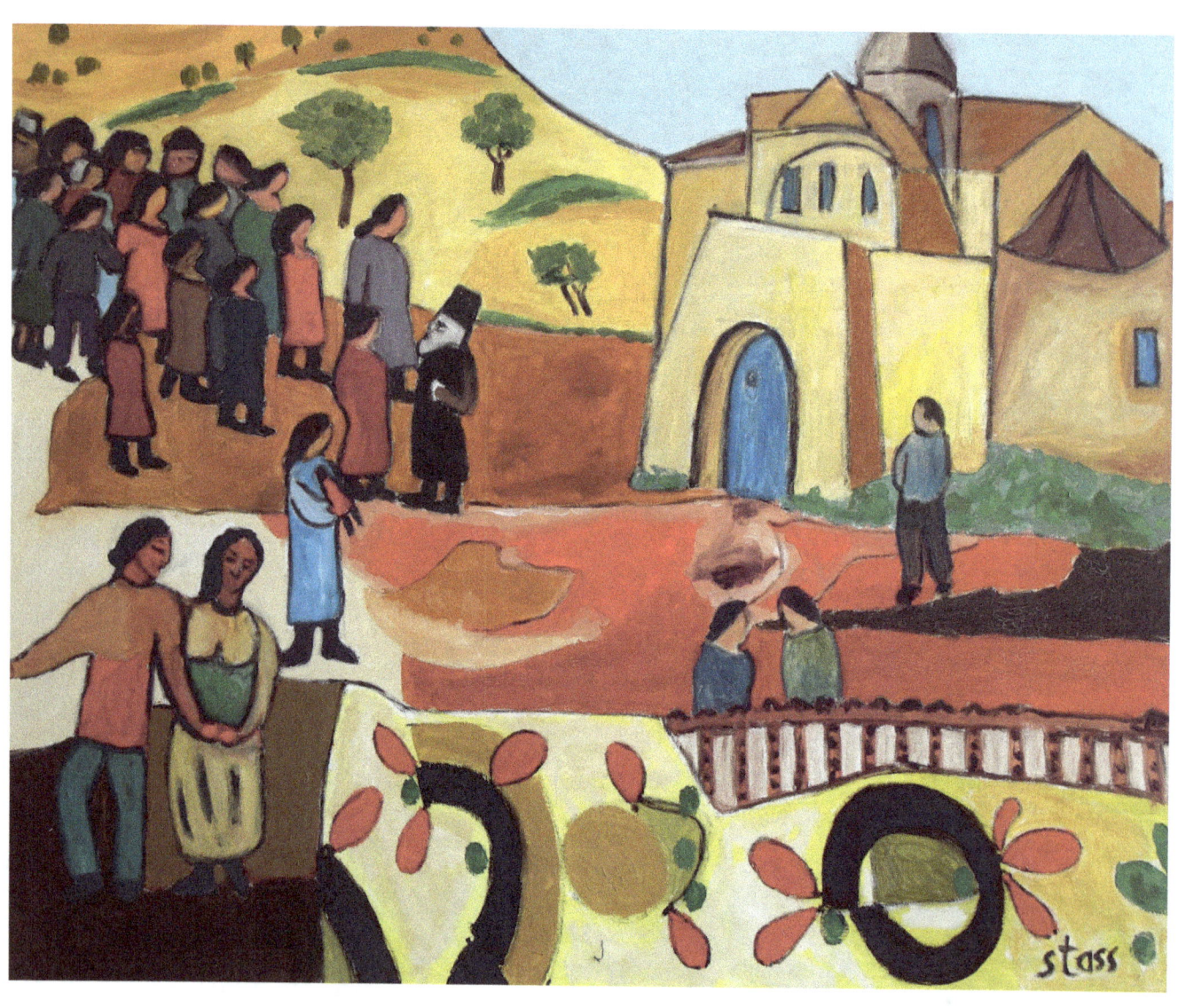

1993

The Priest

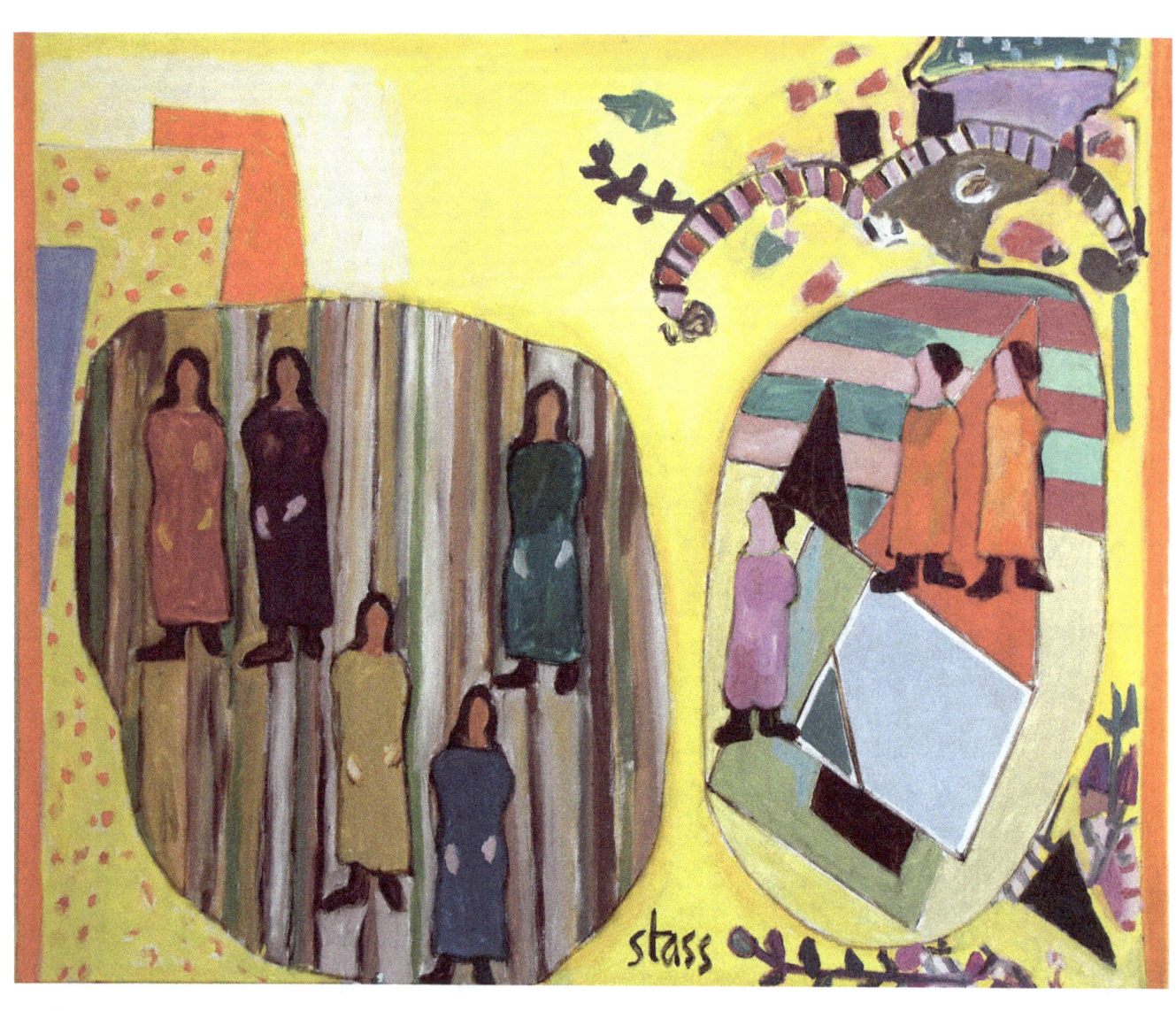

1994

Women in the Fields

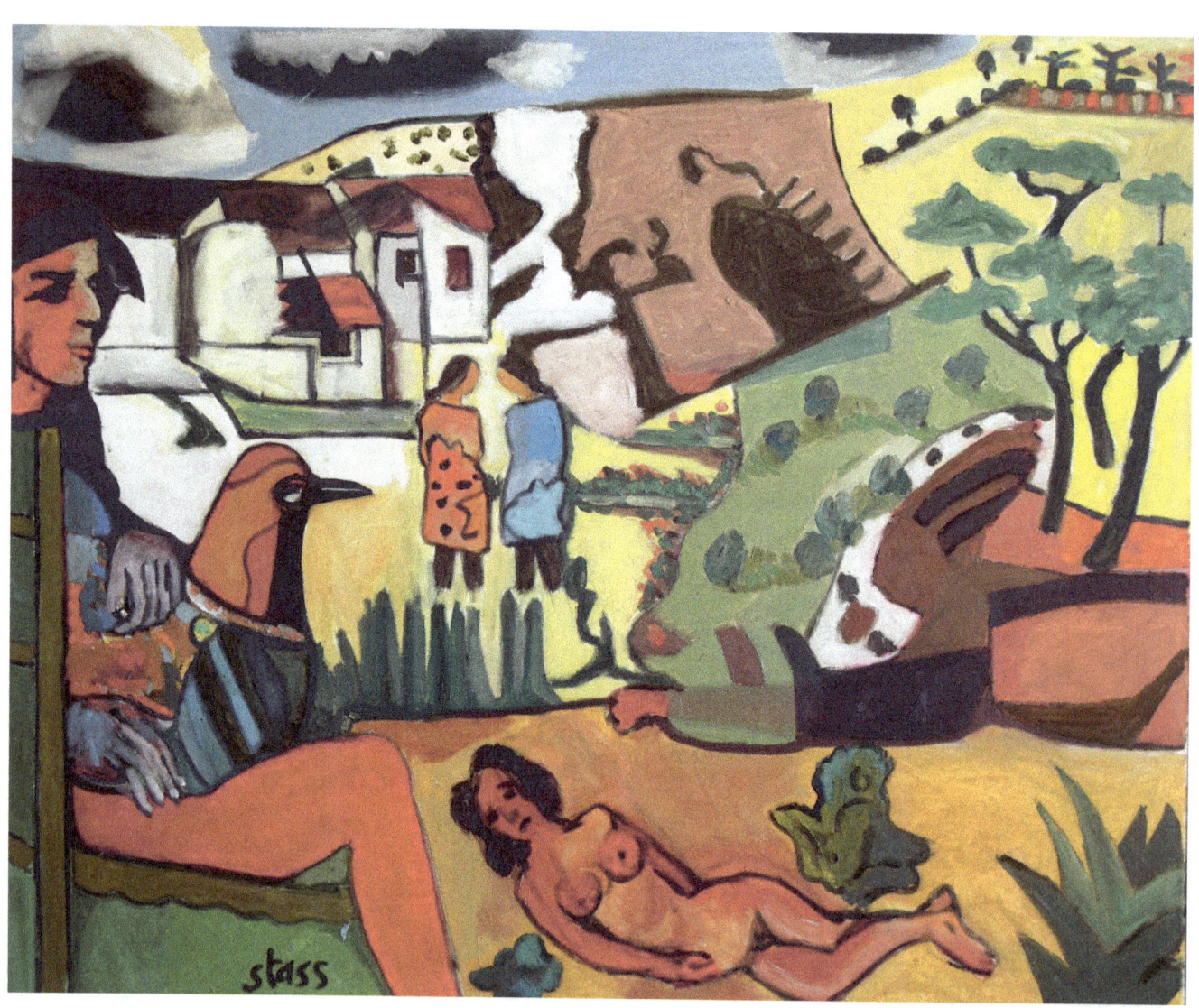

1995
Red Nude

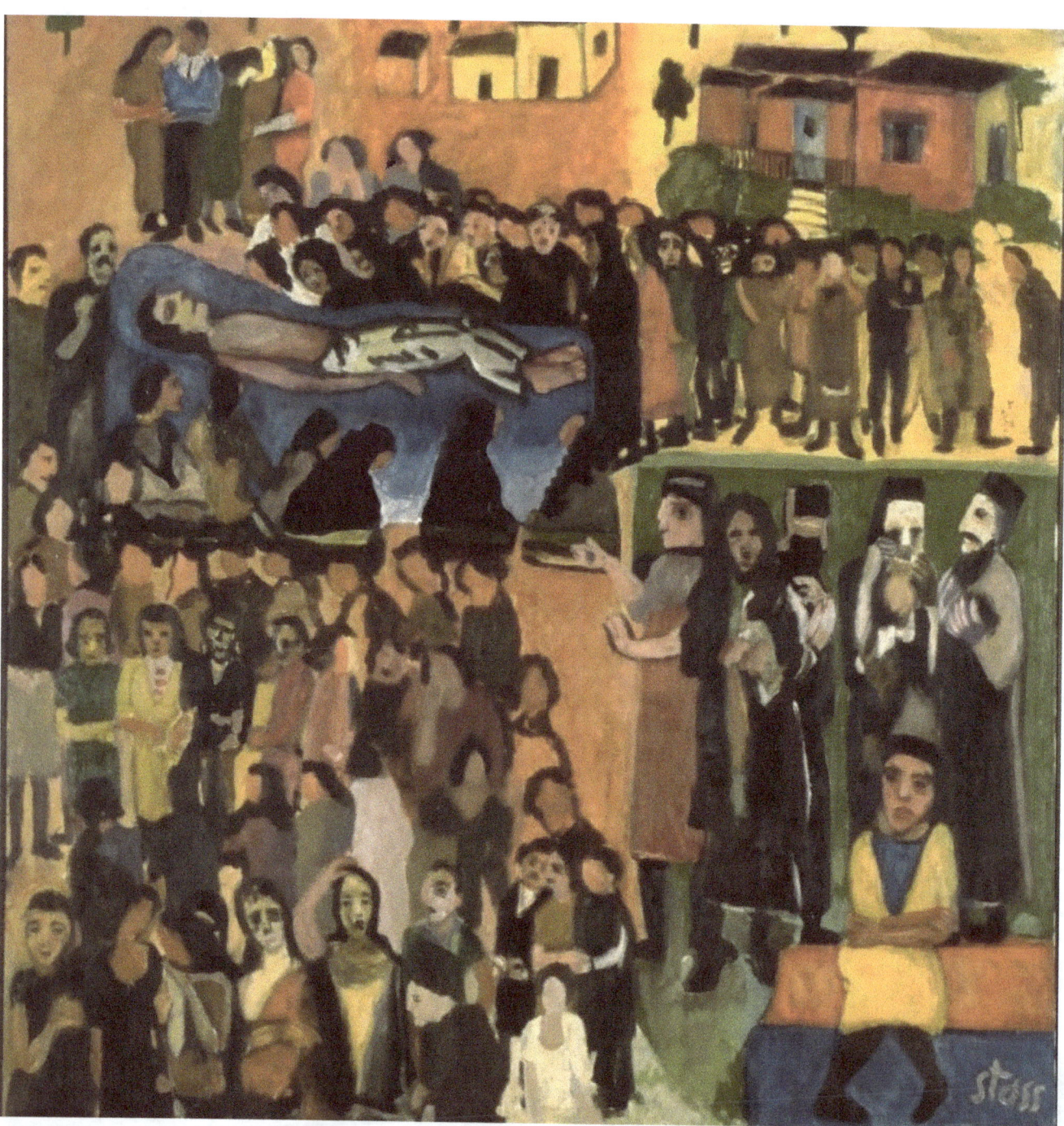

1996

The Murder of Kutlu Adal

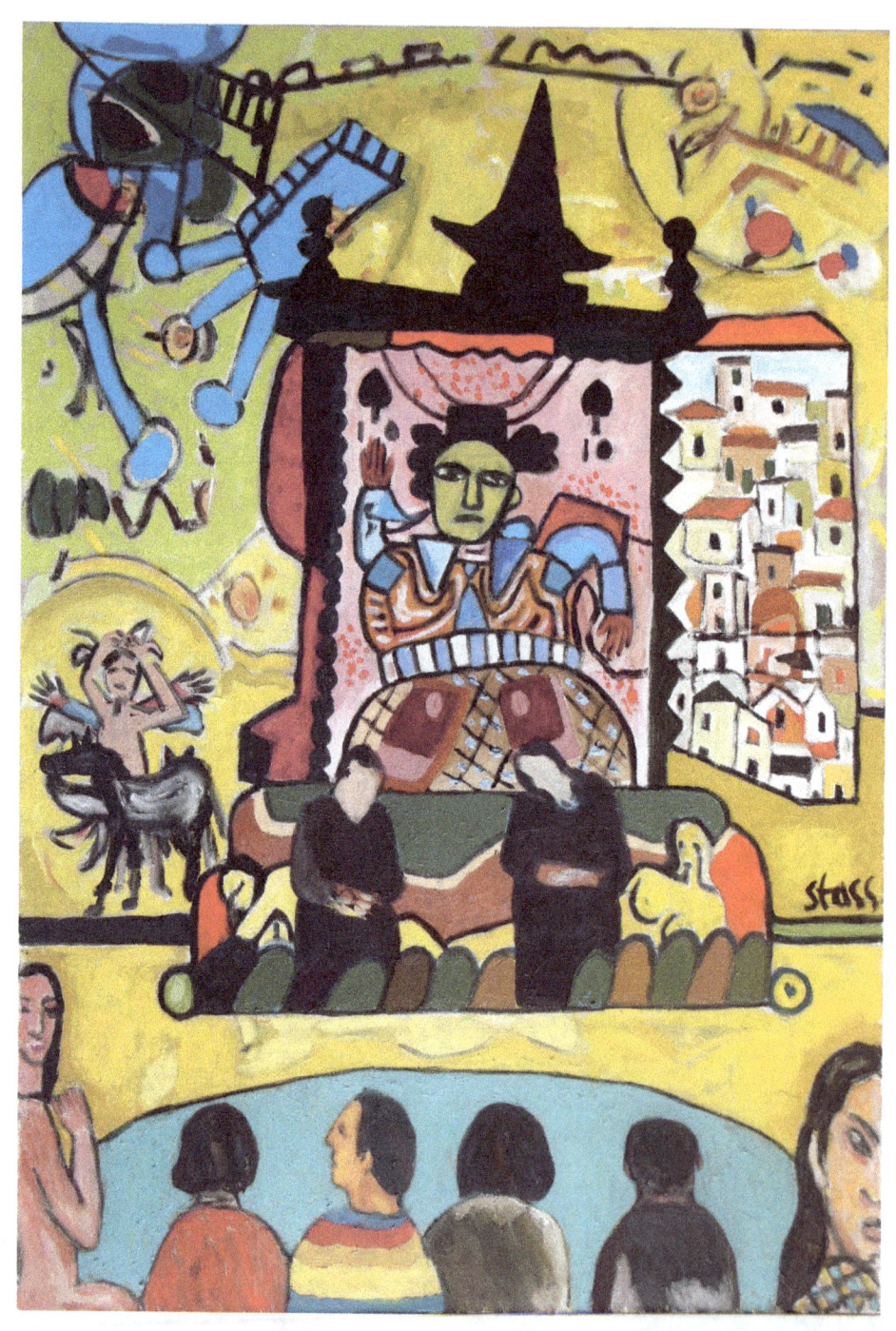

1997
Magical Fantasy

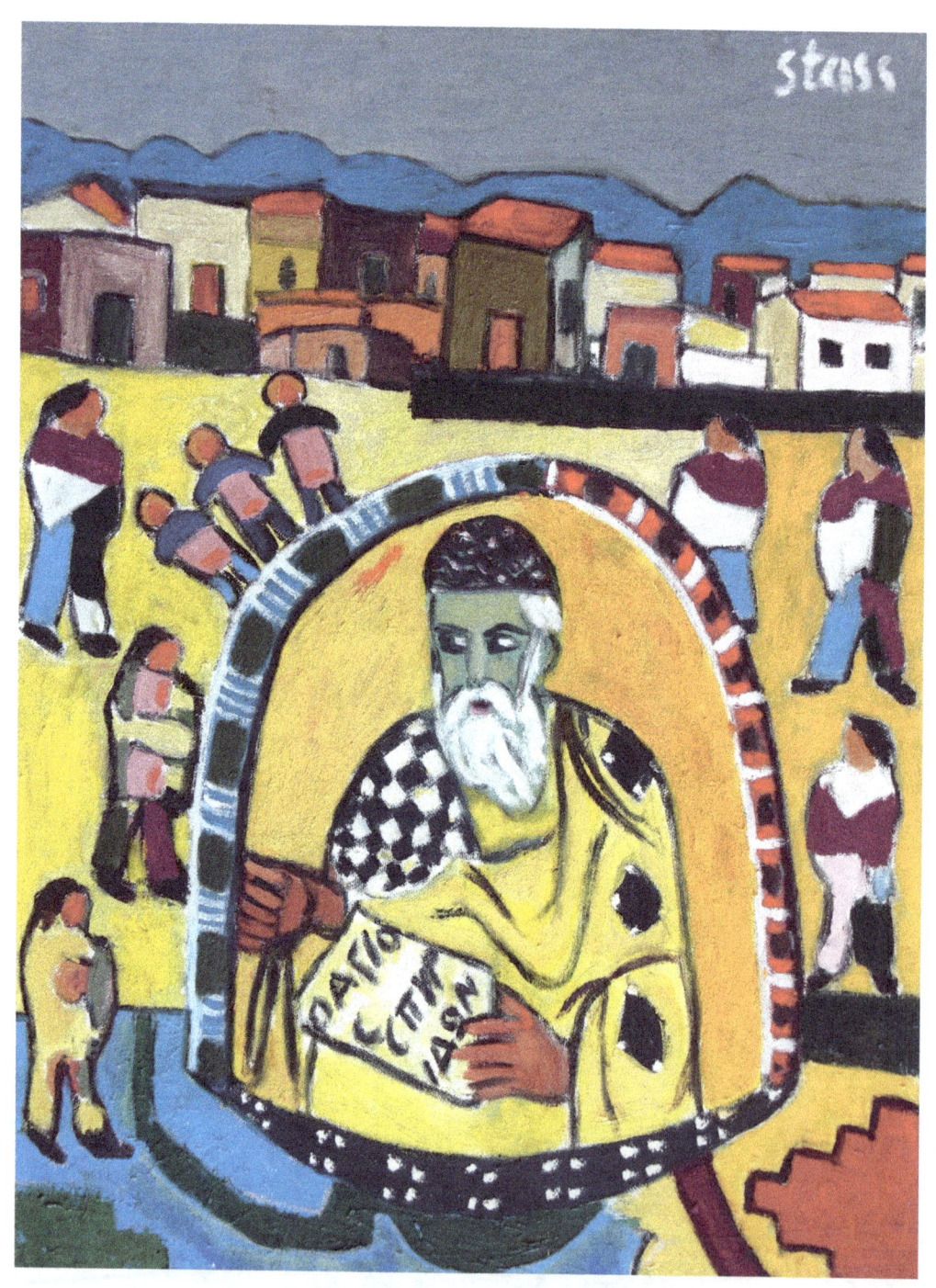

1998
Saint Spiridon

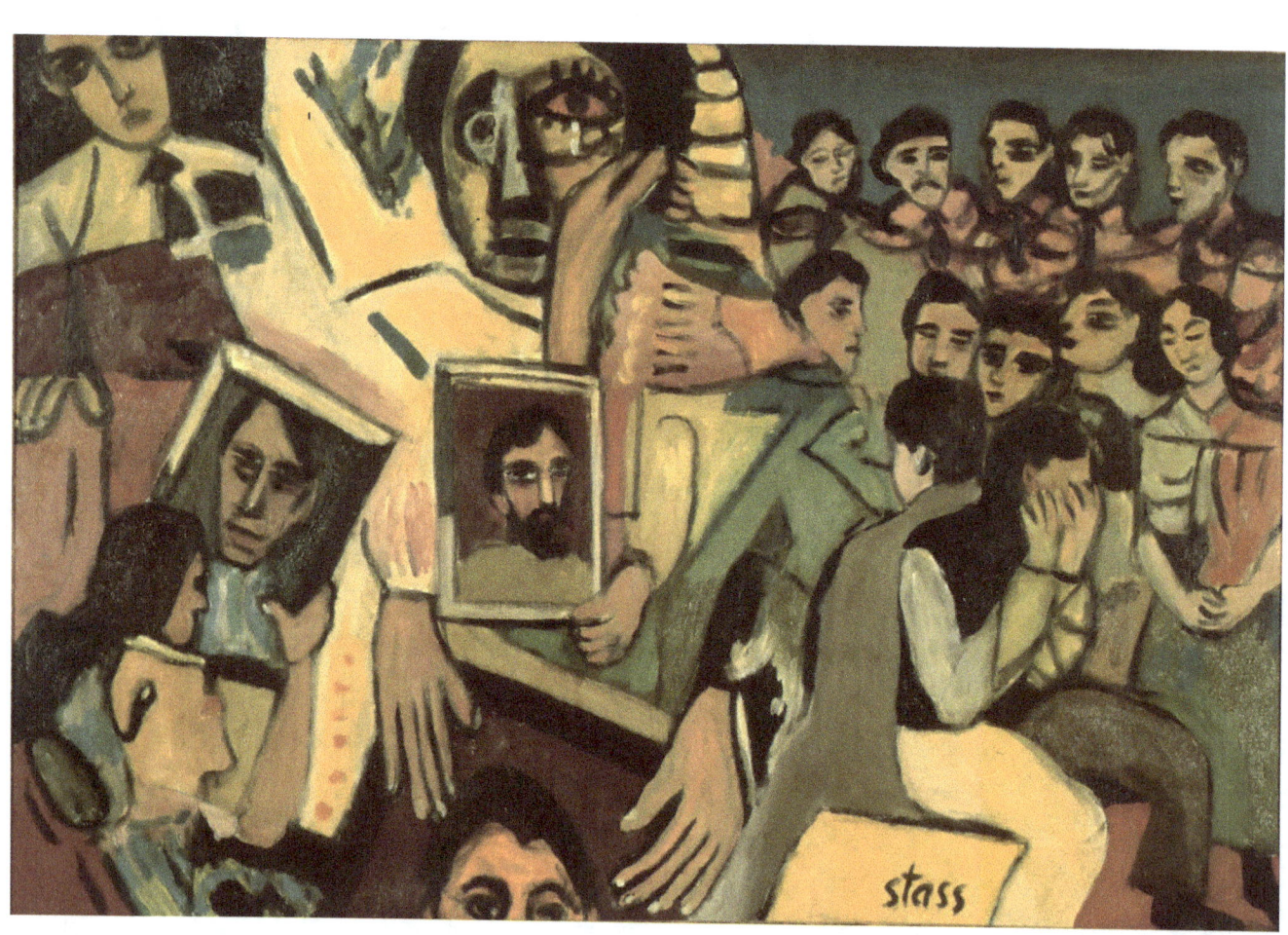

1999

Waiting for the Missing

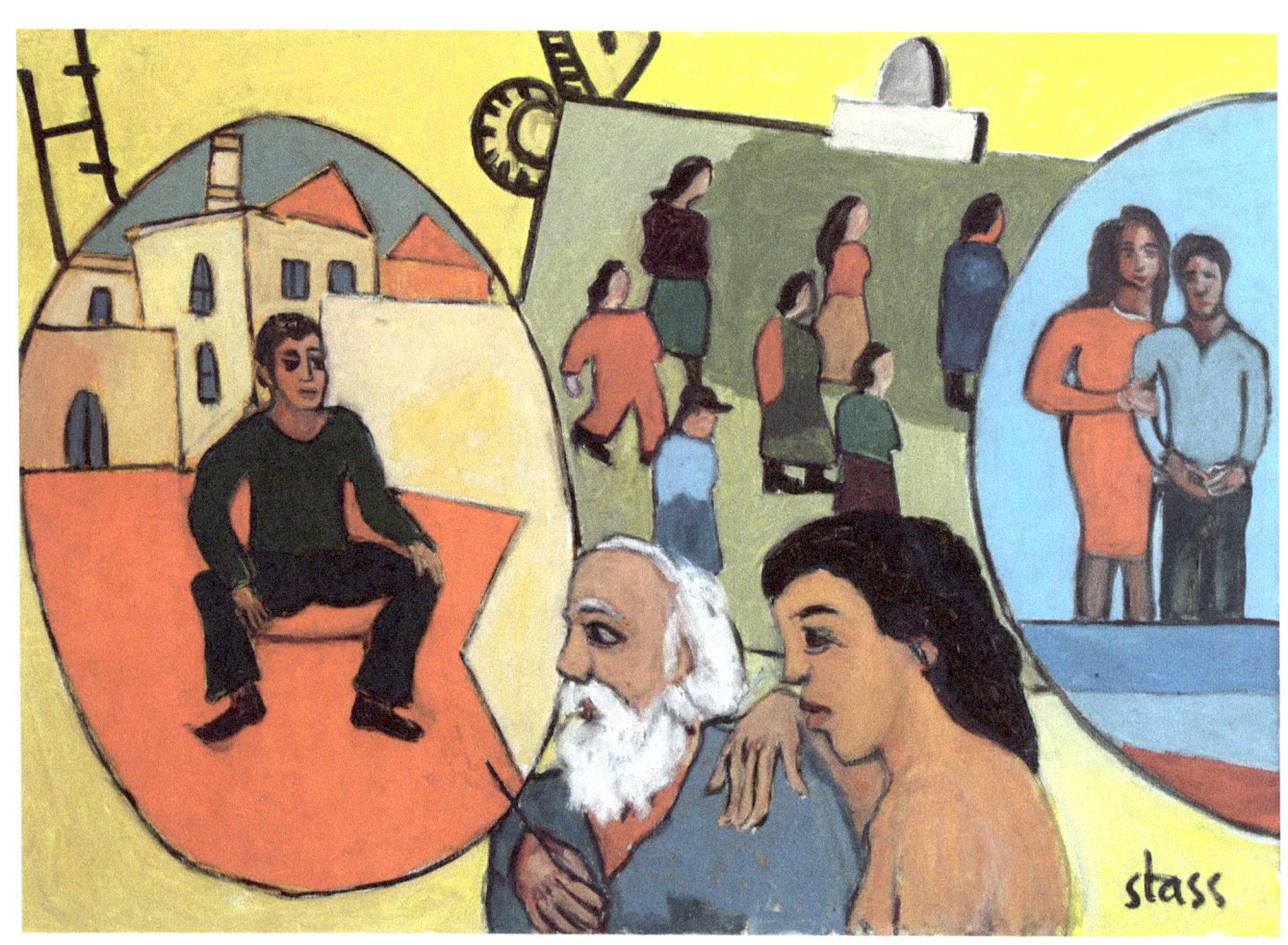

2000
The Artist Remembers

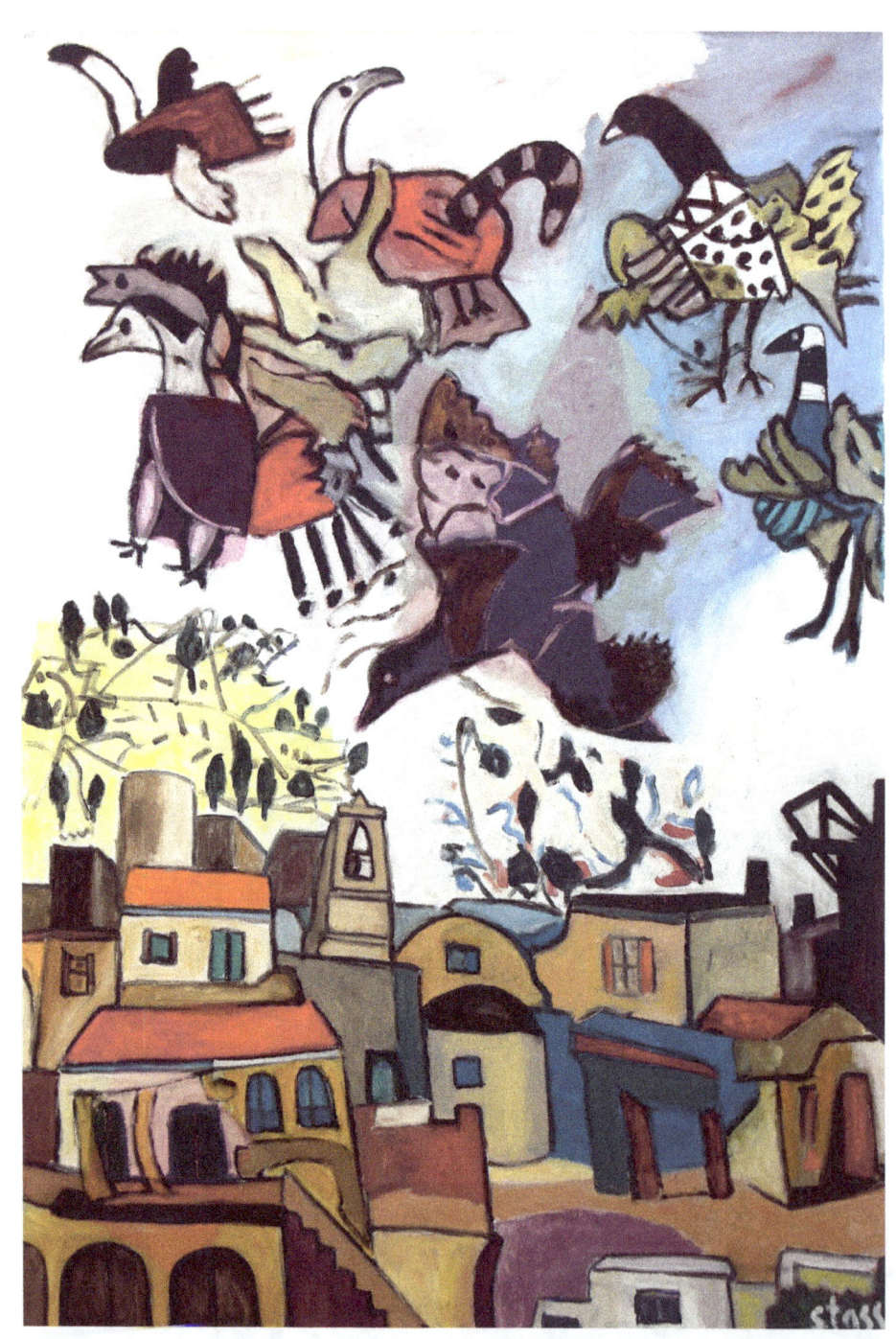

2001
The Birds

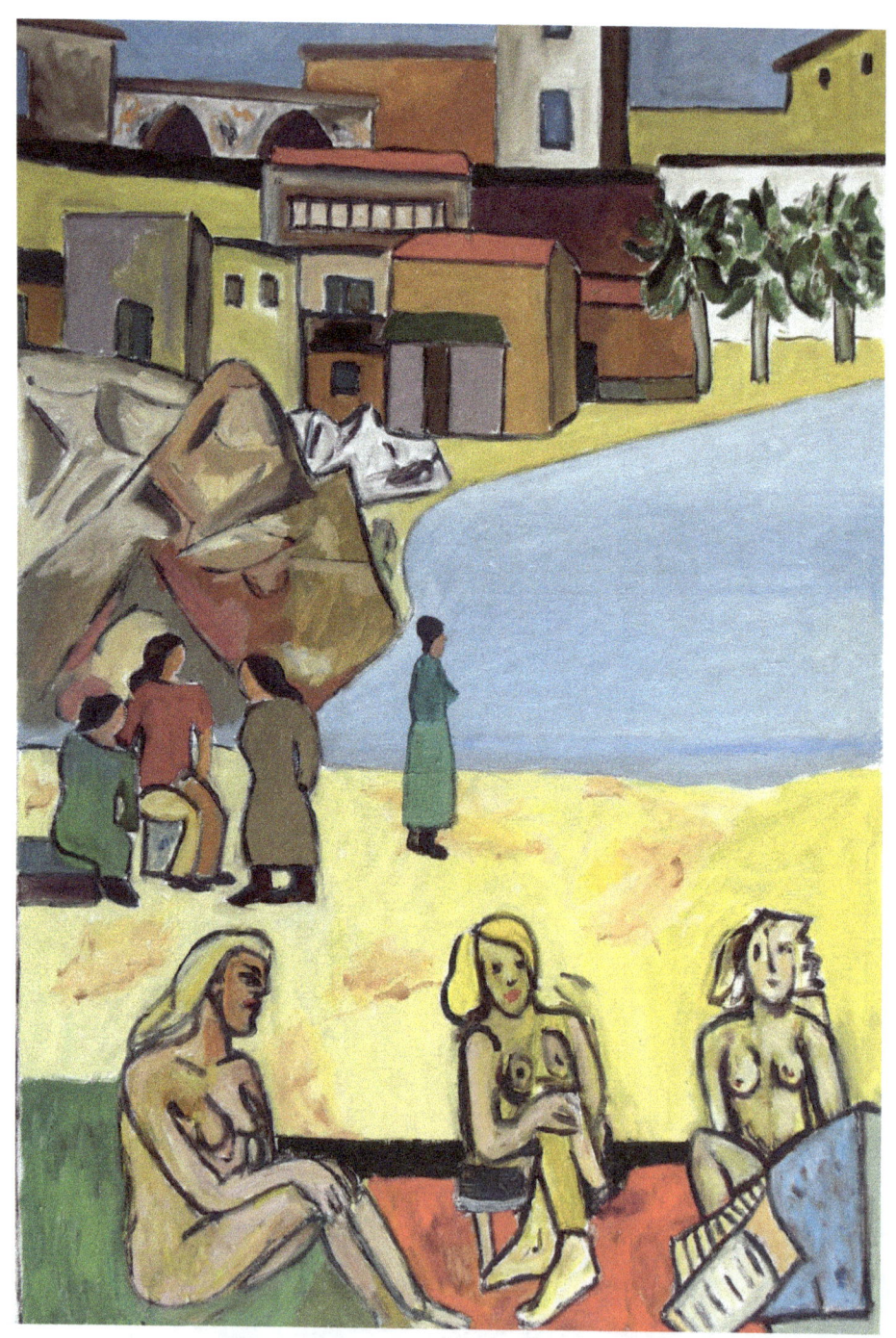

2002
Women at the Beach

A project by the European Capital of Culture

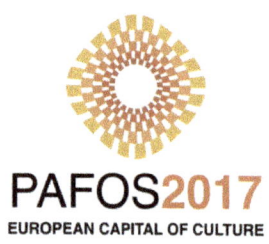 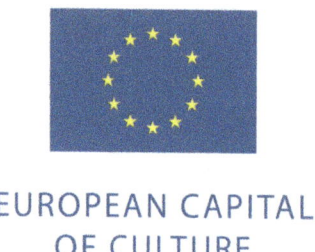 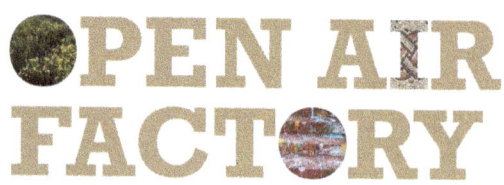

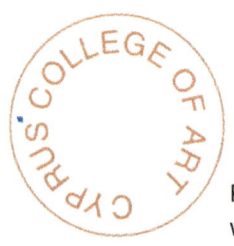

Produced with assistance from the Cyprus College of Art
www.artcyprus.org

www.ingramcontent.com/pod-product-compliance
Lightning Source LLC
Chambersburg PA
CBHW080949170526

45158CB00008B/2425